WEST MIDLANDS
FOLK
TALES

WEST MIDLANDS
FOLK
TALES

CATH EDWARDS

WITH ILLUSTRATIONS BY THE AUTHOR

The
History
Press

First published 2018

Reprinted 2019

The History Press
The Mill, Brimscombe Port
Stroud, Gloucestershire, GL5 2QG
www.thehistorypress.co.uk

British Library Cataloguing in Publication Data.
A catalogue record for this book is available from the British Library.

ISBN 978 0 7509 8539 0

Typesetting and origination by The History Press
Printed in Great Britain by TJ International Ltd, Padstow, Cornwall

CONTENTS

INTRODUCTION

In writing this book of folk tales, I have had the fascinating task of finding the traditional stories that underlie a modern county, and a modern county known for its industry at that.

The West Midlands as a county came into being in 1974, created from parts of Staffordshire, Worcestershire and Warwickshire. The excellent Staffordshire and Worcestershire Folk Tales books in this series have already been written by The Journeyman (Johnny Gillett) and David Phelps respectively; it is possible to find many stories relating to the West Midlands in those books, and I recommend them to you.

At the time of writing, the Warwickshire Folk Tales book has yet to be written, but I have avoided those stories with a Warwickshire flavour which are no doubt better suited to that volume.

So what's left? I surprised myself a little by discovering that quite a lot is left! I have made the acquaintance of Midlands witches (Mollie Mogg and Ode Magic to name two), of colourful Black Country characters (Nanny Piggy and Jacky Ding Dong), of various noodleheads (their stories unfairly attributed to Darlaston), several highwaypersons (Rowley Jack and an unnamed woman) and I have renewed my store of stories about those stalwarts of Black Country humour, Aynuk and Ayli. I have found stories of miners and mining, stories with a supernatural or ghostly flavour, and even the modern version of the folk tale, the Urban Myth.

I mention the Black Country; this is a large area of the county with a character all its own. It was once home to the largest coal seam in Europe, much of it on or near the surface. It is believed by some to get its name from that fact; the coal made the ground black. Samuel Sidney, in his 1851 railway guidebook, wrote:

> In this Black Country, including West Bromwich, Dudley, Darlaston, Bilston, Wolverhampton and several minor villages, a perpetual twilight reigns during the day, and during the night fires on all sides light up the dark landscape with a fiery glow. The pleasant green of pastures is almost unknown, the streams, in which no fishes swim, are black and unwholesome; the natural dead flat is often broken by high hills of cinders and spoil from the mines; the few trees are stunted and blasted; no birds are to be seen, except a few smoky sparrows; and for miles on miles a black waste spreads around, where furnaces continually smoke, steam engines thud and hiss, and long chains clank.

However it may be described, the Black Country did much to give this county its character. The coal deposits and the iron ore as well as fireclay, which were all to be found in the area, led to the region becoming the cradle of the Industrial Revolution. Although the factories and furnaces whose polluting smoke caused the 'perpetual twilight' noted by Sidney are now long gone, and much of the industry is gone too, the people of the Black Country remain. I hope I have reflected their warmth and their humour in this book.

The West Midlands is much more than an industrial county. Much of it is surprisingly rural, and although there used to be a great deal of heavy industry, some of the manufacturing was lighter. Alongside the coal mining, ore mines, chain making and the like was nail making, sword and knife manufacture, gun making, leatherworking, needle making and button making, and I have included stories which weave in and out of the manufacturing and farming history of the county while not in themselves being factually 'historical'.

I have learnt a lot in researching this book, and I have enjoyed writing it. I hope you get as much pleasure from reading it.

Cath Edwards, 2018

ACKNOWLEDGEMENTS

A number of people have given me stories for this book: thank you very much Taffy Thomas, Graham Langley, Paul Butler, David Blythe and Jenna Catton. A whole host of people helped me with their interest and encouragement. My thanks to all of you, you know who you are.

My thanks too to Rhys Jenkins, who helped with collating research, making the task easier.

Last but by no stretch of the imagination least my love and huge appreciation to my lovely partner Paul Fisher, who has been supportive in all kinds of ways.

ABOUT THE AUTHOR

CATH EDWARDS has told stories for over forty years, first as a teacher to children and, in the last ten years or so, to adult audiences. She tells at festivals, in museums, in schools, at storytelling clubs and a host of other venues. Her repertoire is based on traditional folk tales, particularly from the British Isles, and she very much enjoys finding and telling stories that she has heard no one else tell. She runs occasional storytelling training workshops and coaching sessions for less experienced storytellers. She lives in Walsall in the West Midlands and is co-host of Lichfield Storytelling Club, a monthly club for adults. Cath is the Society for Storytelling Midlands representative.

Visit Cath's website at: www.storytellingforall.co.uk

1

Mining and Miners

Around the turn of the eighteenth century, many of the poor working people in the Midlands were close to starvation. The price of wheat and many other basic foods had risen sharply in the preceding decades, such that it was becoming impossible to live. In many areas, Birmingham and Wolverhampton included, food riots broke out, with those suspected of profiteering at the expense of the poor coming in for threats of violence and more.

The threats were occasionally put into writing. A letter sent to a miller included the words:

> *Your family I know not, But the whole shall be inveloped in flames. Your Carkase if any such should be found will be given to the Dogs if it Contains any Moisture for the annimals to devour it.*

In surprising public-spiritedness, local magistrates would often ensure that farmers and millers sold wheat and other foods at an affordable rate, especially at times of shortage. So, the indignation that led a farmer who was also a magistrate to receive the following is perhaps understandable:

We right to let you know that if you do not medetley [immediately]
make bread cheaper you may and all your nebern [neighbouring]
farmers expect your houses rickes barns all fiered and bournd down to
the ground. You are a gestes [justice] *and see all your felley cretyrs* [fellow
creatures] *starved to death. Pray see som alterreshon* [alteration] *in a*
mounth or you shall see what shall be the matter.

These are desperate words from desperate people, and the situation
was no better for the Black Country colliers. There is a story of the
Bilston colliers who staged a more peaceful demonstration of their
plight; it involves Edward Woolley, who also appears in the chapter
'Guns and Edward Woolley'.

Edward Woolley and the miners

Bilston was located on the South Staffordshire Coalfield (as
the county boundaries then were), and while large areas of
the coalfield were near to the surface, in Bilston the coal was
deeper within the earth, and so the Bilston miners had a harder
and more dangerous job to extract it. The perils were real and
sometimes fatal: fire, flooding, choke damp, tunnel collapse and
unhealthy conditions.

The challenges of the work were only moderately rewarded and
with the price of food being as high for the miners as for everyone
else, the men, as no one was doing anything to help them, felt
driven to help themselves. In the circumstances their chosen action,
at least in this story, seems very restrained. They decided to fill a
wagon with coal and drag it the 130 miles to Westminster, to

the Houses of Commons, to draw attention to their plight and to plead their case.

The miners, with their wagon load of coal, were setting out on their journey, making their way through the streets of Bilston in the hope of attracting help and support from the local people in whatever form it might be offered. Instead, they attracted the attentions of Mr Woolley, local businessman and busybody. He was driving in his old-fashioned low carriage, when he caught sight of the ragged procession approaching him. He stood up, reins and whip in hand, and drew himself up to his full, not at all impressive, height, and began to hurl abuse, well peppered with the sort of choice language which the miners may well have heard before but which they were not accustomed to hearing shouted in the street for everyone to hear. For the time being abandoning their wagon, the miners as one man advanced on Woolley; as they neared, he began laying about him with his whip, insulting the men and swearing, if anything, worse than before.

One miner caught hold of the whip and, twisting it out of Woolley's grip, flung it up and over his shoulder, where it flew behind him, skittering along the street and coming to rest some 50 yards away. Woolley turned pale as the men surrounded his carriage. He sat down abruptly and gripped the edge of his seat with white knuckles, as if that would save him. With something that could have been courage or stupidity, he began to threaten the miners, telling them what he would do to them if only he had his old yeomanry sword with him.

By now, a crowd of amused onlookers was starting to gather. They watched as some of the men lined themselves up at either shaft; the pony standing between them rolled its eyes and tossed its head. The other men positioned themselves on each side of the body of the carriage; several hands grasped each wheel. On an unseen signal – the men were after all used to working as a team – the carriage was lifted a little off the ground, and the men at the shafts began to swing them round with the pony shuffling sideways to keep up. To the delight of the crowd, Woolley, with a mixture of rage and fear, was scarlet-faced and raving, shouting to be put down, screaming for his yeomanry sword, bawling now at the audience for not helping him. An old woman stepped forward. She rummaged in the pocket of her apron and found what she was searching for. She turned to hold the grubby handkerchief aloft, showing it to the assembled townsfolk, then, with grandly affected concern and courtesy, she offered it to Woolley 'to dry your eyes'.

Soon the manoeuvre was complete; Woolley's carriage was set down undamaged, its occupant unharmed, but facing in the opposite

direction. One of the men slapped the pony's rump and, accompanied by hoots and shrieks of laughter from the crowd, it trotted smartly back in the direction from whence it and its owner had come.

From that time onwards unkempt street urchins would shout at Woolley when he appeared in the streets: 'Where's your sword, Mr 'Oolley?' At least, that's what they would shout when they weren't shouting the other thing, as related in another story, later in this book.

The miners, sadly, on that occasion found that their project to take coal to Westminster, there to plead their case, was a failure.

There is an old song, 'The Brave Collier Lads', which, as well as exhorting young women to marry miners, contains this verse:

Come all you noble gentlemen, wherever you may be,
Do not pull down their wages, nor break their unity;
You see they hold like brothers, like sailors on the sea,
They do their best endeavours for their wives and family.

In happier times, it was the custom of the miners and other workers to mark the turning of the year with various traditional celebrations. May was a particularly active time, with the warmer weather and promise of summer. May Day, the first Monday of May, was the occasion for a variety of customs and celebrations. Industrial workers would decorate their places of work with branches of May blossom, or hawthorn, which must have been an incongruous sight: pitheads, chimneystacks, foundries, factories and engine houses all wreathed with frothy creamy-white flowers. The buildings of villages and towns, too, would be decorated. Parties of May-gatherers would make off to the nearest woods or even hedgerows, where they cut and collected armfuls of May blossom; returning to the village green or town square, they placed their trophies on the ground for communal use. When all the parties had returned, the branches were shared out and used to decorate the doorways of houses, inns and the church porch.

Some of the boughs gathered must have been quite sizeable; the largest would be chosen to serve as the maypole, and, decorated with ribbons, streamers and garlands, it was propped firmly up on the green to be the focal point of the festivities. The maypole might be 'christened' by the local crier, who, armed with a pot of 'humming ale', would pour part of it over the maypole and then drink the rest. As 'humming ale' is described as 'strong liquor that froths well and causes a humming in the head of the drinker', one might wonder what proportion of the pot was poured, and how much retained to be drunk.

G.T. Lawley collected the following rhyme which describes the christening ceremony from an old resident of Bilston in the mid-nineteenth century:

> *Up with the maypole, high let it be,*
> *If none say me 'Nay!', I'll now christen thee,*
> *The maypole, the maypole, thy name it shall be,*
> *Now all you good folk, come shout with me,*
> *Hurrah! Hurrah!*

Those who had not collected and distributed the May boughs would have been busy with preparations for a shared feast and the construction of the bower for the Queen of the May. The girl chosen to be May Queen was carrying on an ancient folk tradition, but one that might also have been recognised

in some way in the local church. In the words of an anonymous
hymn:

Bring flowers of the rarest
Bring blossoms of the fairest
From garden and woodland and hillside and dale
Our full hearts are swelling,
Our glad voices telling
The praise of the loveliest flower of the vale.

O Mary we crown thee with blossoms today,
Queen of the angels and Queen of the May

O Mary we crown thee with blossoms today,
Queen of the angels and Queen of the May

Their lady they name thee
Their mistress proclaim thee
Oh, grant that thy children on earth be as true
As long as the bowers
Are radiant with flowers
As long as the azure shall keep its bright blue

O Mary we crown thee with blossoms today,
Queen of the angels and Queen of the May
O Mary we crown thee with blossoms today,
Queen of the angels and Queen of the May

The maypole dance is described in a rhyme from Wolverhampton:

All round the maypole we will trot,
From the very bottom to the very top,
Now I've got my Nancy to trundle on my knee.
Oh! My lovely Nancy she's the girl for me.
She hops and she skips while the tabors play,
It's well for the shepherds on the first of May.
First come the buttercups then come the daisies,
Then come the gentles, then come the ladies.
So all around the maypole here we trot
From the very bottom to the very top.

Bands of colliers took part in a traditional May Day dance; one of their number carried a long stick, on the end of which was a collecting box, which he would shake to keep time with the music and to encourage the spectators to make a contribution. All decorated their clothes with ribbons, and the dancers carried stout staves. They were accompanied by a musician, perhaps a fiddler. The dance as described by Lawley sounds like Morris dancing, with rows of four men facing each other, striking each other's staves in time with the music while changing sides. When the miners were on strike and times were particularly hard, the Morris dancing would be a means of raising funds. The miners composed songs that explained their plight; the chorus of one, sung in the mid-nineteenth century, went:

> *O, the shilling!*
> *O, the shilling!*
> *We'd sooner starve*
> *Than go to work*
> *At a shilling a day!*

The May Day celebrations would be completed by groups of colliers, ironworkers and other labourers making their way in to the countryside, where they would enjoy cups of the customary whey drink. The ingredients were simple: milk, which was bought from local farmhouses, and rum, which the workers took with them. They drank toasts to the day with such great enthusiasm that it seems they often made a nuisance of themselves, romping through the lanes and fields, running impromptu races and engaging in equally impromptu pitched battles, their good sense no doubt disappearing at the same rate as the contents of their rum bottles.

THE COLLIERS AND THE BISHOP

One late afternoon, a group of Black Country colliers, all friends, were walking home from the pit along a country lane when they saw ahead a travelling pedlar, riding on his donkey cart. The cart was laden with a great variety of wares: bolts of cloth, metal pans, crock pots, cutlery, scissors, shears, bundles of ribbons, boxes of buttons, nails, tools, farm implements, combs, brushes and what seemed to be an endless variety of other things.

As the friends watched, the pedlar drove his cart over a particularly bumpy stretch; the contents bounced and rattled and when the wheels hit an exceptionally deep rut, a kettle jumped out and landed on the soft grass at the side of the road. The pedlar hadn't noticed, and he continued on his way.

The colliers strolled over to the kettle, and one of them picked it up. It was a perfectly good kettle, and a debate started as to which of them should have it. An important decision should not be hurried, so they repaired to a convenient wall and sat on it to continue their discussion. At length, one of them suggested that they have a tall-tale-telling contest, with the man who told the most implausible story winning the kettle.

John offered to start.

'I was walking through a field last Sunday, on the way to visit my girl. All of a sudden the sky grew dark. I looked up and I saw purple clouds covering the sun and stretching from one horizon to another. The clouds changed colour, from purple to dark green to red to purple again, and then it came on to rain. But it didn't rain ordinary rain made of water. This rain was made of gold and silver nails. Well, it hurt, having gold and silver falling on me out of the sky, so I looked around for somewhere to shelter. I saw a little house and ran towards it. The door opened when I got close so I ran in, and as soon as I was inside the door slammed, the house flew into the air and landed in the village. And that's why I've got a new house.'

John's friends gave this story their fullest consideration, and they agreed that none of it was believable. Then it was George's turn.

'I was in that field last Sunday as well, and I can tell you that everything that John has just told you is absolutely true.'

John at that point had the good grace to laugh. George went on.

'And I walked out of the field and went back to the village where I felt thirsty so I went into the inn. The landlord looked just as he normally did, and he was wearing what he always wears and the inn was exactly the same as it always is. And the landlord says to me, "All right George? What would you like to drink? Have anything you want because all drinks are free today."'

This time, all of George's friends laughed, and they were still laughing when a man on a horse approached. It was the Bishop from the big town. He reined in his horse, bid the men a good afternoon, and asked them what they were doing. They explained that they were having a tall tales contest and that two of them had already had a go, and the rest of them were going to take their turn.

The Bishop frowned.

'So you are all, in fact, telling lies?'

None of them knew quite how to answer that. It wasn't lying, not proper lying, but they didn't know how to say that to a Bishop. He saved them the trouble of replying.

'I am deeply concerned about this. You must understand that lying in any form is wrong, and you must not do it. Why, I myself was brought up not to tell lies from a very young age, as soon as I was old enough to understand, and I can honestly say that I have never lied, not once in my life.'

The colliers tried to keep their faces straight. Then one of them snorted, another sniggered, a third chortled, and soon they had all slipped off the wall and were laughing so hard that they struggled to stand up. The Bishop looked on with undisguised anger at their disrespectful behaviour. John was the first to regain the power of speech.

'Oh, your honour, that's a good one. Here, you better take it!' And he handed the kettle to the Bishop.

2

MINERS, SUPERSTITION AND THE SUPERNATURAL

The job of a miner was fraught with dangers and sadly accidents, injury and deaths were not uncommon. The folk of the Black Country, where the mining took place, were known for being superstitious, and how understandable that miners would be more superstitious than most.

In the Cockfighter's Arms in Old Moxley there used to be a large board in the taproom, above the fireplace, clearly painted with a list of warnings to colliers. Amy Lyons, in her 1901 book *Black Country Sketches*, records the contents:

YE COLLIERS' GUIDE OF SIGNES AND WARNING.

1st – *To dream of a broken shoe, a sure sign of danger.*
2nd – *If you mete a woman at the rising of ye sun turne again from ye pit, a sure sign of death.*
3rd – *To dream of a fire is a sign of danger.*

4th – *To see a bright light in ye mine is a warning to flee away.*

5th – *If Gabriel's hounds ben about, doe no worke that day.*

6th – *When foul smells be about ye pit, a sure sign that ye imps ben annear.*

7th – *To charme away ghosts and ye like: Take a Bible and a key, hold both in ye right hand, and saye ye Lord's Prayer, and they will right speedily get farre away.*

In the same vein as dreaming of a broken shoe is a superstition that to find an old shoe on the way to the pit signifies bad luck; but if the finder can hide the shoe, without being observed, the bad luck is averted. Meeting a woman at sunrise is modified by some into 'meeting a cross-eyed woman', but G.T. Lawley records the following story from 1711:

> Some colliers going to work in Mr Peroehouse's Colliery at Moorfield, near Ettingshall, met a woman. As it was sunrise they became alarmed, and some of them turned back. Several others went to work laughing at such fears. In less than two hours an explosion of fire-damp occurred, and a man was killed.

With such an experience, it is quite understandable that there would be a great fear of breaking a taboo.

The Gabriel Hounds were an invisible air-borne pack of dogs, whose baying could be heard from the skies. Hearing the Hounds on the way to work would make miners turn for home, because it would mean sure disaster. Some sceptics noted that a skein of wild geese taking flight at dawn or dusk and calling to each other across their accustomed arrow-head flight formation, sounded very like

the baying of hounds. Similarly, the Seven Whistlers, who made bird-like cries overhead or at the pithead, caused miners to refuse to work. It seems that all seven have never been heard whistling at once. Up to six have been counted; the belief is that if all seven whistle at once, then the world will come to an end.

The Dead Man's Jacket

In the Black Country, as in many other places, there was a belief that the dead should go to the grave as whole as possible, that is, with all their body parts and with their immediate earthly possessions. To deprive a corpse of a personal item after death was a very serious transgression and would result in the spirit of the dead person walking abroad in search of their property, trying to have it returned.

Two miners, Toby and Edward, were working together in a cramped part of the mine off the main tunnel. With barely room to swing a pickaxe, they found themselves having to work in single file, Edward in front and Toby behind him, each man in turn carrying a load of the coal they had hewn to the skip. So they worked for hours, until it was time for a break. Edward took off his jacket and hung it on a nail in one of the pit props, remarking how warm it was getting. The two men sat down side by side, took the lids off their snap tins and began to eat their sandwiches. Toby was the younger man, as yet unmarried, and he looked up to Edward, who had that calm steadiness of personality that inspires confidence.

Toby unscrewed the top of his water canister. 'How long have you been a miner, Ed?' he asked.

Edward thought for a moment. 'Fifteen year come Michaelmas.'

'Will I be earning like you do one day, Ed?' Toby had to give his parents much of what he did earn, and it didn't leave him a lot for savings or for buying warm clothes.

'Be patient, lad,' was Edward's advice. 'I couldn't buy a nice thick jacket like that one,' he nodded toward the pit prop, 'not for a long time. Your turn will come. Better get back to work now. The more coal we send up, the more money we'll get.' He rose to his feet, securing his snap tin, and turned towards the coalface. He never spoke to Toby, or anyone else, again.

Once more, Edward took the lead in the narrow tunnel, and, only half an hour later, that was what saved Toby from the worst of the blast. The older man's body was thrown back onto him, knocking him to the ground and banging his head hard against the pit floor, but also shielding him from much of the heat and pressure of the explosion. Other miners working in adjoining tunnels came running to do what they could: Toby, apart from being dazed from the blow to his head, was unharmed, but Edward was beyond help.

Edward's body was carried from the mine with as much care and dignity as the conditions allowed, and he was returned to his family. Toby was carried, too, though he remembered little of it. For him, the whole episode seemed dreamlike and vague.

In those long-ago days, little was understood of the effects of shock, and so it was that Toby was expected to return to work after only a day at home recovering. He joined a team of three other men, working a natural cavern off the main tunnel, only 30 feet or so from the site of the fatal blast. Toby worked silently. Every blow of his pickaxe was a struggle and he found himself jumping at every sound. When the crew stopped for a break, he couldn't bring himself to join in the conversation and instead, taking his lantern, he wandered away along the tunnel. He came to the narrow working where he and Edward had been together so little time ago. He stood transfixed, looking at the litter of coal and rock thrown down by the explosion, then his eye was caught by something. Hanging on a nail on a pit prop was Edward's jacket.

Without any thought at all, Toby walked over to it and lifted it from its hook. He held the rough fabric to his face, and breathed in. A warm human smell. He slipped the jacket on over his own thin one, went back to the cavern and carried on with his work.

It was the same day that he first caught sight of the miner. Only his back, and only for the briefest moment before he disappeared around a corner. Again, as Toby and the team were leaving for the surface, he saw someone, further back along the tunnel, just beyond the light cast by his lantern. He called to his teammates to stop, there was a miner still in the tunnel who should come up with them. One of the men, more understanding of what Toby had suffered than was his employer, went back to take Toby's arm.

'Come on, lad, there's no one there.' He led Toby after the other men towards the main shaft.

Over the next two days, Toby saw the strange miner more and more. He kept feeling he was being watched as he worked, and when he turned round he would see only the briefest glimpse of a man turning away into the darkness. When the men sat down for their snap, Toby often had the sense that there were five of them, not four. He would see out of the corner of his eye, next to him in the lantern light, the toecap of a boot, a snap tin resting on a knee, an arm clad in a shirt sleeve, but jerking his head to catch sight of the elusive miner, he would see only the rock floor and the coal wall.

Late on the second day, feeling too warm, he took off Edward's jacket and laid it down. Bending to pick up his pickaxe, he caught sight again of a boot, where no man was standing. He straightened up so quickly he felt dizzy, and when he saw it he had to put out a hand to steady himself. The likeness of his old workmate was standing, only a few feet away, looking directly at him. The spirit had its thumbs tucked into its belt, just like Edward used to do, and it did not speak, but simply dropped its gaze to the jacket, looked again at Toby and faded gradually from view.

Toby collapsed to the floor and was carried once more by his workmates to the surface. 'I knew it was too soon for 'im to come back, but the boss won't listen, will 'e?' he heard one of them say. He was taken to his parents' house and put to bed.

The next day, in spite of his mother's best efforts to get him to stay in bed, he got up, dressed and picked up Edward's jacket. He took it to the house of Edward's widow, and, with much sorrow for what he had done and many apologies, he returned it to the family. What the grieving widow thought of this is not known, but from that time Edward's spirit seemed able to rest and was never seen above or below earth again.

White Rabbit and Old Nicholls

The previous story told of a dead miner's spirit returning to the mine, and there was widespread belief amongst miners that restless spirits as well as devils and imps of evil intent were commonplace below ground. Even the benevolent mine-dwelling fairies, the 'knockers' or 'tommy-knockers', who were known to make a tapping noise to warn miners of danger, and who would band together and help the colliers with their work, with their own little picks and shovels, could also take offence and turn against the miners, hide their clothes and tools and steal their candles.

Because of the absolute belief in the reality of these supernatural entities, the miners often called on the services of local 'wise men' or 'white witches' to advise the men of how to secure protection, or even to go down the mine themselves and exorcise the evil spirit. One such 'wise man' was known as White Rabbit; his real name is lost to history. The local colliers had seen an evil-looking apparition while working in the heart of the mine, and they were afraid to go back there, believing they were in great danger from its malevolence.

White Rabbit went to the pithead and executed a number of occult signs. He instructed the miners that a party of brave volunteers must go down the mine at midnight to the area where the spectre had been seen and the leader of the party must carry the Bible in his right hand and a key in his left. He gave them a number of further instructions.

The miners went into a huddle and debated who should go. A man nicknamed Caggy because he was 'caggy-onded' (left-handed) was elected to be leader because of his level-headedness and general good sense. Four others eventually volunteered, and the whole group took themselves off to The Chainmaker's Arms to pass the time and imbibe a little Dutch courage. They left the inn in good time to find their way to the centre of the mine by midnight.

At the pithead, those staying above ground took charge of the winding gear, and the volunteer exorcists began their descent into the underworld. Emerging from the shaft into the tunnel, and led by Caggy with his Bible and key, they began chanting as they had been told to as they advanced along the level:

> *Matthew, Mark, Luke and John,*
> *Bless the errand we're come on.*

They followed this by reciting the Lord's Prayer in unison, then began the whole process again, constantly chanting as they approached ever closer to the centre of the mine. There it was!

Glowing with its own ghastly light, the spectre drifted towards them from the far end of the tunnel. Chanting faster and louder, the men watched in terror as it came ever closer, unaffected by their incantations and emanating an air of evil and threat.

Suddenly one of the men shouted out, 'Caggy! You fool! You got the Bible in the wrong 'ond!'

Sure enough, Caggy was holding the Bible in his left hand. As the evil spirit was almost upon them, Caggy swapped the Bible to his right hand, and the spectre vanished, never to be seen again. White Rabbit's reputation remained intact.

The story is a little different for the next 'wise man', however.

In another mine, the colliers had a problem that was annoying rather than threatening. They kept supplies of candles in the pit tunnels, so they could always be sure of being able to relight their lanterns if they were burning low, but the candles were disappearing at a great rate. The miners thought it might be due to the tommy-knockers who had for some reason taken offence and were taking their revenge, so they consulted their 'wise man', Old Nicholls.

Old Nicholls used the utmost of his occult powers to divine the cause, and he announced that there was a devil in the pit that was stealing the candles. He gave the miners instructions, which were not unlike the advice that White Rabbit gave in the previous story.

A party of men went down the mine, one of them carrying the Bible, and all of them with matches in their pockets. They were to recite the Lord's Prayer backwards at any sign of an evil presence.

The men stationed themselves near to a stack of candles, since that was what seemed to be attracting the devil, and settled down to wait in the dark. They waited and waited, and eventually they began to hear something – a faint scratching sound. Was it the devil's hoofs scuffing on the floor? His claws searching for the candles? The man with the Bible opened it, and so that he could read from it, the others reached for their matches, at the same time wondering what horrors the light might reveal.

The first man to strike his match held it up – and the light showed dozens of rats scurrying away.

Old Nicholls' reputation took a bit of a knock that day.

THE MINERS' FRIEND

This story was given to me by Graham Langley, who has done a great deal to promote storytelling across the Midlands for many years.

A long time ago, it was the custom for one of the pit foremen to stand at the pithead, handing a token to each man who descended into the mine. Each token was numbered, and the foreman wrote the number and the name of the man in a ledger. When the miners reappeared at the end of their shift, they handed back their token and the foreman checked off the man's name, so that if a miner did not emerge from the pit when expected, they would know who it was they were looking for.

Two miners were starting their shift, and they took their tokens as usual. They went down the shaft in the cage, stepped out at the bottom with their lanterns ready, and started their walk along the tunnel to the face they were currently working on. It was a long way, and they were about halfway when they became aware of

someone behind them, hurrying to catch them up. It was a man, older than them and a stranger.

They greeted him in a friendly way, partly because they were like that, and partly because in their line of work lives could depend on men co-operating and looking out for each other. The older man returned their greeting and fell into step beside them.

'Don't think I've seen you down here; have you worked this pit before?' asked one of the younger men.

'Not for a while,' replied the older man. They walked on in companionable silence, nearer and nearer to the coalface.

Then the older man stopped dead. 'No further lads.' He listened for a moment. 'Not much time. Get out. Get out now!' He grabbed their arms, swung them round and started running. Wasting no time with questions the younger men ran too, and by the time they had nearly reached the shaft they had overtaken him. Then they heard a roar far behind and below them – the unmistakeable sound of a tunnel collapsing. Without thinking, they scrambled into the lift cage and tugged on the rope to signal that they wanted to come up, but the moment they reached the surface they shouted to the foreman that they had to go back down, there was a man down there. What name had the foreman written in the ledger?

'Steady on lads,' said the foreman. 'There's no one else down there. I've been here the whole time, and I only sent you two down.'

3

Short Midlands Stories

The following are a collection of short stories that the people of the West Midlands have been telling one another in pubs, at work and at home for decades and, in some cases, centuries.

A Crooked House

A long time ago, houses built near mine workings often became undermined, literally, by the gradual extension of the tunnels below. The houses, often inhabited by miners and their families, were rented from landlords who seemed to care little for the welfare of their tenants.

One such house had tilted as the ground shifted under it. The tenant miner wasn't too worried by the slope of the floors; the main drawback was that he was going bald because every time he slid towards the bottom of the bed in the night, his wife dragged him back by his hair, but he wasn't too worried by that. No, the problem was that the whole family was disturbed by the large numbers of black beetles and crickets which infested the house. From dusk to dawn, the cacophony of scratchings and chirrups which came from behind the fire grate had to be heard to be believed.

The miner asked the landlord to do something about the problem several times to no avail. Then he had an idea. In those days, new pit areas were often opened up by blasting, the explosives being made with loose gunpowder. The next day at work, the miner helped himself to what he thought would be a sufficient amount to remove the pests, or at the very least to give them something to think about. Trickling the powder into the back of the fireplace, he stood as far back as he could and set light to it.

Emerging, wheezing and coughing, from his house with his face even sootier than was usual after a shift down the pit, the miner went to call on the landlord, persuading him to visit the house to see what had happened. The landlord stood and stared for a few moments at the fire grate and mantelshelf, now positioned in the centre of the room, before he asked, 'What happened?'

The miner nodded sagely. 'You wouldn't think it would you? That even thousands of insects would have the strength to do that. But see for yourself!'

TWO CROOKED HOUSES

In centuries past and in the days before building regulations, houses built for workers could be thrown up with little care for quality; walls were thin, chimneys were shared between adjoining houses, roofs sagged. A near neighbour of the miner who had the problem with the insect infestation was in the impossible situation of having a house that filled with smoke every time a fire was lit in the grate. At length, the landlord paid a visit to see what was wrong with the chimney.

He arrived as a chimney sweep, engaged by the frustrated householder, was at work. I remember myself, as a young child, being asked to go outside the house and to shout when the sweep's brush emerged from the chimney, and the same was asked of the son of the tenant.

For anyone who has never seen a chimney sweep at work, the process is this: the brush is wheel-shaped and it has a rod a few feet long fixed to it like an axle. The sweep has a number of rods, all with brass threaded fittings each end and he or she adds extra lengths as needed, pushing the rods, with the brush on the end, up the chimney from the fireplace inside the house. With the boy outside, then, watching the chimney top, and the door open, the sweep was screwing on section after section and shouting to the boy, 'See anything yet?'

The boy kept shouting back, 'No, nothing!' The boy was quite right, and the sweep was perplexed because he knew roughly how many sections he needed for the height of the house. The sweep, the tenant and the landlord were all considering this issue when the woman from next door stormed through the door, in quite a fury.

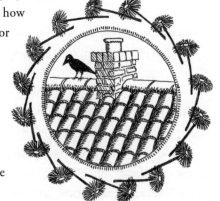

'What do yo' think yo'm doin'? Yo' know my old mon works the nightshift down the pit. 'E's tryin' to sleep, and yo've pushed 'im outer bed three times!'

A 50/50 CHANCE

Some Cradley Heath chain-makers had been on a bit of a spree one night. The next morning they all just about managed to drag themselves out of bed and make their way towards the workshop, meeting each other one by one as they trudged along the road. When they were all assembled, they looked at each other blearily with bloodshot eyes. Glancing towards the workshop, one spoke for all: 'I dunno if I can face a day of 'ommerin' iron. I doh think my 'ed'll tek it!'

The others nodded lugubriously. What to do? Then another man had a suggestion. 'Let's get an 'ommer and throw it up in the air. If it stays up there, we go to work. If it falls down, we goo 'ome.'

The wisdom and indeed the fairness of this course of action was agreed upon, the hammer was procured and with due solemnity on the part of the workers it was rendered airborne. The result? The law of gravity remained unchanged.

REVENGE

One of the chain-makers of the last story was returning home in the early hours following his spree with his mates (the women chain-makers, I should add, had more sense). He was trying to fit his front door key into the lock. It would do him no good because when he had not come home by midnight, his wife had drawn the bolt across the door. The local constable on his nightly rounds, seeing the difficulty the man was having, stopped to ask him if he was all right. The man assured him that he was, and the constable continued on his way.

Two hours passed and the constable once more arrived at the chain-maker's house, to see him sitting on the front step. The constable enquired again, 'Are you all right, sir?'

The man grinned. 'I am. I couldn't get the door open, so I knocked. She didn't answer, so now I'm makin' 'er wait.'

THE LEG

A well-to-do lady living on a small estate had a Black Country cook. One evening the cook brought a roast chicken to the table. After the meal, the lady called the cook and complained that the roast chicken only had one leg. Clearly, temptation had got the better of the cook and she had eaten one of the chicken legs and the lady was expecting a confession of guilt.

The cook asked the lady to come out to the kitchen garden where the chicken coop was to be found, then madam would see that *all* the chickens had only one leg. Due to the time of day, the hens were roosting and it did appear that the cook was right. The lady, not to be fooled, flapped her hands and said, 'Shoo! Shoo!', and the birds, unsettled, each showed their second leg.

The lady turned triumphantly to the cook. 'There! What do you say now?'

'Ah, now, that's all very well,' said the cook. 'But I doh think yo' shooed the one on the table, did yo'?'

CATCHING THE HORSE

It was winter, and a cold and frosty one at that. One evening, the farmer sent his young son out into the field to put a bridle on the horse. The boy fumbled about in the dark for a while, the placid animal's breath making clouds of steam all around him. Eventually, he gave up the struggle and went back into the farmhouse.

'I can't do it, dad,' he said. 'It's that cold out there, I can't get the bridle over 'is 'ead, 'is ears have frozen.'

The farmer frowned. It had never, to his knowledge, been that cold before. He lit a lantern and went out to see for himself.

When he got to the field, there was the horse. Calmly chewing the cud.

DOWN AT THE STATION

A young woman hurried onto the platform of Stourbridge Town station, just in time to see the train pulling away. She stamped her foot in frustration and said to the porter, 'Oh! I really wanted to catch that train!'

The porter gazed down the track after the departing locomotive and said (this was in the days when public safety was given far less consideration than it is now), 'Well, it's a slow train. I bet if yo' run, yo' con catch it up.'

So that is what the young woman did. She took off down the track in pursuit of the train and was soon lost to the porter's view.

Twenty minutes later she reappeared, breathless but smiling. The porter observed, 'Yo' didn't catch it, then?'

'No, not quite, but yo' should have seen me mek the blighter puff!'

Buying the Ring

A Walsall saddle maker had been courting for some time and he felt it was the right time to 'pop the question' to his beloved. He walked the short distance from the workshop to the jeweller's in Stafford Street. He went in and spent some time looking at the displays of rings, munching thoughtfully.

The owner came across to ask if he could help, and the man explained he was looking for an engagement ring.

'Eighteen carat?' asked the jeweller.

The saddle maker couldn't see that it was any of his business, but answered anyway: 'No, as a matter of fact I'm chewin' tobacco.'

The road

A Solihull 'lord of the manor' guarded his land jealously and was constantly on the lookout for trespassers. One day he was on his horse, riding around his property, checking the fences, when he saw a woman carrying a basket of washing walking right across the middle of one of his fields. He urged his horse on and rode up to the woman at a canter, drawing to a halt only a foot or two away.

The man glared down at her. 'Now look here, my good woman, you are on my land.'

She smiled up at him, shifting the laundry basket on her hip to a more comfortable position. 'I'm doing no harm, and this is a heavy load to carry the long way round.'

The landowner did not return her smile. 'This is typical of you people! Don't you understand that this is my land? Surely you noticed that there is no road across this field?'

The woman turned to look behind her at the way she had come. 'No, there isn't, neither,' she said. She patted his knee comfortingly. 'No, there's not much of a road, but for you, love, I'll put up with it.' And she walked on.

By the Sea

A Dudley family had saved hard for a holiday and were excited to arrive at the seaside. They carried their suitcases from Rhyl station to the boarding house and then the children, a girl and a boy, were clamouring to go and see the sea. So they all trooped off along the promenade and across the sand until they found a likely spot. They settled down on a picnic rug in the sunshine and the parents helped the children wriggle into their swimming costumes under cover of a towel.

The boy was very keen to go and paddle. His mother thought he was too little to go on his own, so his older sister offered to go with

him. Mother and father both began
to relax and enjoy the warmth
of the sun and the gentle sea
breeze, until suddenly the
woman realised that she
hadn't been watching the
children. Shading her eyes
and looking out over the
wide expanse of sea, she could
only see her daughter's head and
shoulders above the waves.

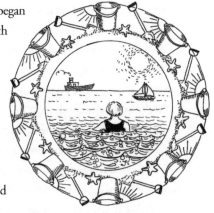

"Where's Tommy?' she shouted.

'Don't worry, mum,' the girl called back, 'I'm 'oldin' 'is 'and!'

ANOTHER WATERY TALE

The winter was unusually cold, and two brothers had gone skating
on Sarehole Mill Pond. The older brother returned home not too
long after.

'Where's Timmy?' asked his mother.

'Well, it's like this,' said the boy. 'If the ice is as thick as he
thinks, he's skating. If it's as thin as I think, he's swimming.'

THE GRUMBLING FOREMAN

Two friends were working on a building site in Gornal. Over their
dinner break, they were discussing their foreman.

'I dunno,' said the first man. ''E doh seem to like anything I do. Everything's wrong, according to 'im.'

'Ar, I find the same,' said the second man.

'If I'm sweeping up, I'm not quick enough. If I'm diggin' a 'ole, it's not deep enough. If I'm carryin' bricks, I should be carryin' more.'

'Well,' said the second man, 'do what I do. Swear at 'im.'

Their sandwiches finished, they returned to work. They met again the following day at dinner time.

The first man was angry. 'I thought yo' told me to swear at the foreman! I tried it like yo' said, an' he's told me to go. I lost me job!'

'Yo' did it wrong! Yo'm only s'posed to swear at 'im when 'e's not there!'

ACCURATE BOWLING

Kings Heath cricket team were playing away at Erdington. A loyal band of supporters had accompanied them to the match and were dismayed at their team's performance. The home team were batting and scoring run after run while no wickets were falling.

The Kings Heath team's followers became more and more disillusioned and disgruntled, until one man said to his mate, 'Our bowler's very good, isn't 'e? 'E's gettin' the ball to 'it the bat every time!'

A DEATH IN THE FAMILY

A worker at an iron foundry was sadly killed in an accident at work and his body was laid out in the bedroom of his home. The foundry owner came to visit the widow and her children to pay his respects.

Settled in the front room with a cup of tea, he began to hold forth to the family about the good qualities of his former worker.

'Such a diligent and hardworking man,' said the foundry owner. 'Always ready to go the extra mile.'

The widow smiled. 'Was he? That's nice.'

'Oh yes. A very willing worker. Kept calm under trying circumstances.'

The woman said nothing.

Warming to his theme, the owner said, 'He had a cheerful word for everyone.'

The widow's mouth set in a thin line.

The man concluded, 'So helpful towards his workmates, too. Giving encouragement where it was needed, and he'd lend an ear to a mate with troubles.'

The woman could contain herself no longer. She turned to her daughter. 'Sarah! Will yo' go upstairs and check if it really is your father!'

HAM AND EGGS

Bill and Eddie had been working together down the mine when they were cut off by the collapse of a section of roof. They had waited for two days now, listening to the sounds of their mates' picks and shovels on the far side of the rockfall, digging them out.

To keep their spirits up, they talked of everyday things.

'I reckon it'll be about dinner time now, Bill,' said Eddie.

'Ar, I think yo'm right,' agreed Bill.

'If we 'ad any eggs, we could 'ave 'am an' eggs.'

Bill brightened. 'Could we, Eddie?'

'Ar, we could,' said Eddie. 'If we 'ad any 'am.'

A NAUGHTY BOY

A Gornal mother had a large family and her youngest son was particularly troublesome. To get a bit of peace at the weekends and in the hope that he might learn better ways, she enrolled him in Sunday School.

The Sunday School teacher also found him unruly in the extreme, and in exasperation she told him that he must remember that he can't hide anything from God, because God can see him being naughty.

'In fact,' she said, 'He can see everything.'

Without pause for thought, the boy said, 'Con 'e see our front door?'

'Oh yes,' was the reply. 'Of course He can see your front door.'

'Con 'e see inside our 'ouse?'

Seizing the opportunity, the teacher said, 'He can see inside your house and He can see when you're naughty inside your house!'

The boy asked, 'Well, con 'e see down in our cellar?'

'Absolutely He can, I keep telling you He can see everything.'

The boy was triumphant. 'Well yo'm a liar then, cos we 'aven't got one!'

ON THE DOLE

In 1930, workhouses were abolished. Benefits paid to the unemployed were known as 'the dole', and those who did not qualify for the dole could get help from the Public Assistance Committees.

Bob was now in late middle age, but he had managed to dodge work for almost the whole of his life. He was fit and well, but he was highly skilled in finding reasons for being unable to work: bad back, raging toothache, unexplained headaches, vertigo, ergophobia – the list went on. All his family and friends, indeed virtually everyone in the town, knew he was swinging the lead, but of course no one would 'dob him in' to the authorities.

One day Bob was complaining to his neighbour that he had been taken off the dole and had been put onto Public Assistance, but now the Committee was reviewing his case and there was some likelihood that they would recommend that his payments be stopped.

The neighbour, a hard-working man, pointed out that Bob didn't really have much to complain about; he had, after all, been receiving money for doing nothing for an extremely long time now.

'Well that's my point!' said Bob with some heat. 'They want to cast me off after they've had the best years of my life!'

TWO EXAMPLES OF GALLOWS HUMOUR

A man saw his friend walking down the street, almost hurrying.

'What's the rush, Bill?' asked the man.

Bill stopped. 'Oh, I'm off to the doctor's. It's the wife.'

'Is 'er ill, then, Bill?'

'No,' said Bill. 'I got 'ome and I found 'er 'anging.'

'Well, what did she say when yo' cut 'er down?' asked the man.

'She day (didn't) say nuthin',' said Bill. 'I ay (haven't) cut 'er down yet.'

'Why 'aven't yo' cut 'er down?'

'Well, she wor jed (wasn't dead).'

A woman came home and found her husband hanging from the rafter by a rope tied round his middle.

'What on earth?' she said.

The man smiled weakly. 'Doh try an' stop me, I'm 'anging meself.'

The woman snorted her derision. ''Anging yerself? Yo'm supposed ter put the rope round yer neck, yo' fule!'

As he gently rotated, the man gave her a pitying look. 'Well, course, I tried that, day (didn't) I? But I damn near choked meself!'

4

THE GILBERTSTONE

Blakesley Hall in Yardey, Birmingham, is a well-preserved Tudor house with an orchard of heritage apple trees and attractive gardens. When I visited recently, I was shown round by a very knowledgeable volunteer guide. The house itself is fascinating and offers a window into the way people used to live through the ages, but for the purposes of this book, it was the orchard that interested me, because the orchard is the current home of the well-travelled Gilbertstone. There is more about the Gilbertstone later, but first a small digression.

HOB'S MOAT

South of the road named Hob's Meadow, and north of Castle Lane in Solihull lies a small area of oak woodland named Hob's Moat. Some local people call it Bluebell Woods, and those flowers are certainly there to be enjoyed in the spring, but the woods' main distinguishing feature is indeed its moat. To see it, and walk along it, the moat appears like a wide, deeply sunken lane between the trees in the bare earth of the woodland, and it follows a roughly square route. This is what remains of the moat of a medieval fortified house; archaeologists found the remains of a wooden stockade in the outer bank, and in the central area of land enclosed by the moat, charred remains of the manor house and the foundations of a stone tower. Eight hundred years ago it was owned by the Odingsell family, also known as the Hodinsells, which led, it is supposed, to the contraction Hod's Moat which in turn became Hob's Moat.

That may all be true, but I prefer the following story.

Farmer Gilbert and the Hob

A long, long time ago, Birmingham was but a small market town and all around it were farms, woodlands and tracts of open country. A man named Gilbert owned a farm 5 or so miles to the south-east, and like the other farmers in the area, he loaded his wagon with goods to sell, and drove to the market on most Thursdays.

Gilbert, spending most of his time in the quiet and isolation of his farm, was fascinated by his trips into the town. Buildings stretched from Digbeth and Deritend to the Bull Ring on the green in the centre, where the market site was overlooked by St Martin's church. Beyond that, all along the High Street, more shops, houses and businesses all in timber-framed structures where hundreds of people lived and worked. As Gilbert drove his wagon to the market place, he passed workers bent over their benches in the window of the button-maker; he turned his head from the pungent scent of the leather works; he listened to the piercing 'tap-tap-tap' from the house of the metal workers, sounding to the farmer very like the call of the robin that greeted him every morning in his yard.

And in the market, what amazing sights greeted Gilbert's eyes. He sold vegetables, corn and sheep, all in the right season, and so did the other farmers, but there was so much more: coal, millstones, salt – and wonders! Even in those far-off days, people were selling in Birmingham market astonishing exotic goods from abroad. There were stalls with spices, mellow and fragrant; silks in gorgeous colours that were quite dazzling to a country farmer; there were almonds, pottery, wine and even, alongside the local apples, damsons and pears, sometimes bright oranges and pomegranates.

Gilbert did well enough at the market. Birmingham had a growing population to feed, and his fresh goods were welcome. But his eyes were drawn to the other sellers who had such tempting displays. If his wife had a dress made of silk, the other farmers would see how important he was. If he was seen to drink wine, not the commonplace ale and mead, wouldn't it give him stature?

One day, he was returning from the market in a thoughtful mood. He had made a little money and bought a few goods – a new pair of work boots, strongly stitched with linen thread in a shop not 200 yards from the Bull Ring, some lamp oil and, a small indulgence, a block of fine white soap. With more money, he could have bought some of those things that were so tempting but out of his reach. Drawing into the farmyard, he gazed across the fields to the far boundary of his land. At this distance it was hard to see the stone, but he knew it was there, straddling the border between his land and that of his neighbour, Jacob. By some trick of the land's deep fabric, Gilbert's farm was passable for crops and pasture but it was poorer than he would have liked, while Jacob's fields grew better crops and sustained lush green pastures. It drained the life out of Gilbert to see a mediocre return for his efforts when, if only the boundary was different, he would have an easier and a richer life.

That day, standing in his farmyard, he made a decision. He would save all the money he could and then, when he had a good bag of coin, he would buy the field that bordered his land, the field beyond the stone, Jacob's field. Forgetting to mention his plan to Jacob was not the first mistake he would make in the matter.

So it began. Gilbert was a tall, strong man, but the extra work he did on the farm to scrape a little more money out of it wearied him. His wife was hurt and insulted by his constant insistence that she be ever more frugal, when she had already considered herself to be a skilled household manager, wasting nothing and creating much, whether it be cheese, rugs for the floor or clothing, by her own hand. The warmth between them cooled, and their bond became weaker. Thus it was that Gilbert, formerly unremarkable, began to be known by his neighbours and in Birmingham as a man with a surly temper.

Perhaps it was Gilbert's manner that worked against him the day that he finally had enough money in the bag to take across the fields to Jacob's house. He hammered on Jacob's door; if Jacob was surprised at Gilbert's visit, he did not let it show. Inviting him in, Jacob led his visitor to the large kitchen table and poured him a mug of ale. Gilbert drank it off in a few rushed gulps, banged the mug down on the table and pulled the bag of coin from his jacket pocket. 'Here. Payment for that field that's next to my land.'

Jacob smiled gently and pointed out that the field was not for sale. Gilbert's face grew red and, opening the bag and emptying its contents onto the table, insisted that his money was good.

Jacob smiled again. 'Come. Let's collect up your money,' he said, scooping it back into the bag, 'and take a walk together. View the land.'

Jacob led his neighbour out of the house and across the fields. 'So, this is my field. There, beyond the stone, is yours. If we turn now and walk up the hill, we will see further.'

Gilbert was unsure what the man was driving at, but he followed until they were both standing on the farm's highest point. Jacob turned to the south. 'There, that woodland. It's a distance away, but it's yours, isn't it? I'll sell you the field you want for the bag of silver and those woods. That's my offer.'

Gilbert's stomach clenched. 'Those woods? But they're oak, and you know it. The timber's worth a lot more than your field will ever be. Those woods are my pension!' He turned and strode away, back to his farm, and no deal was made between the two men, then or ever.

Gilbert's anger, hot and hard, stayed with him that day and was still smouldering when night fell. He stalked out to the barn, found a heavy fence pole and marched grimly across his fields towards Jacob's property. At the border, he stopped and searched up and down a little way. He found it, the large heavy stone, the boundary stone. He dug the pole into the earth at the stone's base and began to heave. Nothing happened. He tried again, and again, but even though he strained as hard as he was able, he could not shift that stone in the slightest. It was when he was resting his forehead against the pole, trying to catch his breath, that he heard it. Laughter. Light, snickering laughter. He looked up and found himself eye to eye with a strange-looking creature, seated comfortably on top of the stone. The little man had a soft cap on his head, a belted jacket, knee breeches and stockings, and soft leather shoes. His eyes were bright, searching Gilbert's face even as he laughed.

The hobgoblin spoke: 'You seem to be trying to move the stone.' And he again dissolved into snorting chuckles.

Gilbert stood, his mouth hanging open.

The little man continued: 'You won't move it. I think you've found that out. But I can. Tell me where you want it, and I'll move it so it looks like it's always been there. Tell me, how much land do you want?'

Gilbert dumbly gestured toward the middle of his neighbour's field. The hobgoblin turned his head to look. 'Yes, I can do that. But you must agree to give me your wood to be mine to live in. The wood and all the trees in it.'

Gilbert, hanging on as best he could to some sense of reality, considered the hobgoblin's words. It was certainly cheaper than gaining land at the price of the wood and the bag of silver. He could hardly believe he was making a bargain with one of the little folk, but he blurted out that he agreed.

He found himself, the next morning, warmly in bed without remembering how he had got there. He was struggling to assemble vague memories of the events of the previous night when he heard a thudding at the front door. Hastily dragging on his breeches, he stumbled down the stairs and opened the door. There stood Jacob.

'You moved the stone! The boundary between my land and yours! You moved it!'

Kicking his feet into his boots, Gilbert pushed past his neighbour, strode out into the yard and made his way across the fields, followed closely by Jacob. Frowning as he reached the spot where the stone had previously rested, Gilbert saw that there was no sign that anything had ever been there. There it was, some distance away, on Jacob's land. But when the two men neared the stone, Gilbert laughed.

'It's always been here,' he said. 'You've been dreaming.' And he pointed to the base of the stone, which had grass and flowers growing up around it, and even a tendril of ivy that had rooted to it.

'Before us is your land,' said Gilbert, 'and behind us is mine.' And he turned and made his way home, grinning.

Jacob, of course, did not give up straight away. He appealed to other farmers for judgement, but they simply pointed out how settled the stone appeared, and that there was no evidence of any disturbance on the surrounding earth, as there would be if a heavy stone had been dragged. So Jacob had to admit defeat, but he never spoke to Gilbert again.

For his part, Gilbert found that his fortunes did revive a little. He still had the bag of silver, and with his newly stolen tract of land, he began to make a profit. And one day, he was unexpectedly offered money by a timber merchant for a number of apple trees that were no longer any use for fruiting. When the merchant was loading the felled wood onto his cart, he mentioned the woods he had passed on his way. He offered a fair price for three of the oak trees, and without thinking Gilbert agreed.

When a week later the timber merchant returned to fell the oaks, Gilbert was standing by to watch. As the man's axe fell, there was a shriek from deep in the woods. The man paused briefly, 'There's a fox up to no good!' and he carried on striking the tree.

The three trees were finally loaded onto the cart, and Gilbert, the payment still in his hand, turned for home as the man drove away. But making his way along the accustomed path, he tripped over a large stone that seemed just to appear under his feet, and the money scattered amongst the wayside bushes and grass. Gilbert scrabbled in the dirt on his hands and knees, but no matter how hard he searched, he could not find the money. Not one coin.

From that time on, more and more stones appeared on the farm. Fields became near-impossible to plough, the hay meadow became so rocky that Gilbert broke his scythe, and walking on paths that had once been smooth became difficult and dangerous.

The boundary stone, one moonless night, returned to its original position.

Gilbert's house and farm is now long gone. Gilbertstone is a residential area of Yardley in Birmingham. A little further to the south, though, the woods are still there. Hob's Moat. Hob's Woods. A recent survey counted 286 oak trees in the woods. Should that have been 289?

The Gilbertstone itself has in fact travelled about the south Birmingham area over the last century or so. It marked for many years the old county boundary between Worcestershire and Warwickshire, and Gilbertstone House, built in 1866-7, which had the Gilbertstone in its grounds, continued the tradition by not only crossing the Worcestershire/Warwickshire boundary, but also its grounds crossed over into Sheldon, Yardley and Bickenhill; indeed, the stone marked this meeting point. By 1900, it seems that the stone had been all but forgotten and it was hidden amongst some bushes. There it stayed until 1937, when the house was demolished and a local vicar took up the stone's cause and had it moved to the Coventry road for all to see. In 1952 it was moved to Lyndon Green Junior School, where it was again forgotten, lost in long grass until being revealed once more in 1965. In the 1970s it was finally removed to Blakesley Hall, where it sits in the orchard with a plaque giving some of its history.

Gilbertstone House was built on the site of a small farmhouse. Whose, I wonder?

The Gilbertstone is composed of hard volcanic rock of the kind found in North Wales and quite unlike the local sandstone. It is an erratic, carried to the Midlands 12,000 years ago in a glacier.

That may be true, but I prefer the following story.

THE GILBERTSTONE GIANT

Eight hundred years ago, in the reign of King John, a giant lived in North Wales. He loved his homeland, but he had heard stories from travellers of the wonders of the English Midlands, the heartland of the nation. So he resolved to find out for himself if the stories were true. He set out on his journey but hesitated when he reached the borders of the home he knew. Did he really want to leave? Then he had an idea. He would put a pebble in his pocket, as many walkers do, and if he ever felt homesick, he could take it out and look at it. He searched around for something suitable, and at last found a stone that would fit his hand nicely when he reached into his pocket. He picked up the boulder, pocketed it, and off he went.

He marched through Welsh forests and over hills, striding from Betws-y-Coed towards Rhydiydan, on to Cerrigydrudion, then Llantysilo and Llangollen. On and on he went, splashing through the River Dee, towards Oswestry, a detour around Shrewsbury, through Wellington where he bought a new pair of boots, further south to Wolverhampton, through Bilston, Wedgebury and West Bromwich, a pause to peruse the amazing goods on sale in Birmingham market, then a little further south and east, where he sat down. This was the spot. Gently sloping hills, woodland, green as far as his eye could see. He fished in his pocket, brought out the boulder and set it down carefully. He had found his new home, and so had the stone.

THE WARSTONE

I include this little snippet of a tale by way of contrast. It concerns another erratic (or so they say) boulder in Birmingham, the Warstone. Since it was deposited in the Ice Age, it does not appear to have been moved, and it can be found next to the entrance lodge of Warstone Lane cemetery. This in itself is an atmospheric place, well worth a visit for its Victorian catacombs and ancient headstones.

The Warstone sits on a stone plinth, on which are carved the words:

The War Stone

This felsite boulder was deposited near here by a glacier during the Ice Age: being at one time used as a parish boundary mark. It was known as the Hoar Stone of which the modern Warstone is a corruption.

It was recorded in 1390 as marking the boundary between the manors of Handsworth, Birmingham and Aston; it was illegal to move boundary stones, and so it has remained in place.

There is, of course, a story that explains its location, and this story has twice as many giants as the Gilbertstone legend.

There was a giant living in a castle in Birmingham who was the social inferior of the giant resident in Dudley Castle. For years the Birmingham giant had served the Dudley giant, doing his bidding in many ways: collecting rents, digging out silted-up streams, fighting off invaders and whatever else the Dudley giant wanted. Over time, the Birmingham giant's lands began to be more profitable and the giant became prosperous, so much so that he began to ask himself why he was paying court to the Dudley giant. Having asked himself the question, the answer followed quickly: Why indeed?

So the Birmingham giant paid a visit to the Dudley giant and told him, with not a little petulance, that he would no longer be a servant. The meeting did not go well. Whether it was what was said, or the way it was said, or both, we will never know, but the result was that tempers flared, insults were hurled, and finally, as the Birmingham giant concluded that discretion was the better part of valour and scuttled back home, a rock was also hurled, by the Dudley giant, with some force, after the retreating Brummie. The rock landed where we now find it, in Hockley, now famous as the home of Birmingham's Jewellery Quarter.

The rest is history, and there is indeed a little history to underpin the story. Dudley Castle, in its stone-built form, is there to be seen today. But many of England's castles were originally earthworks surmounted by a wooden structure, and there is an eighteenth-century record of a moated site near the junction of Vyse Street and Warstone Lane, believed to be the castle of Sir Thomas de Birmingham. The tale of a spat between two giants may well point to the site of a castle in Birmingham.

5

MAGPIES, CROWS AND OTHER BIRDS

A RIDDLE

Creator of harsh cries I am,
A thief but never tried I am,
A soarer through the skies I am,
Conspicuously pied I am.
What am I?

(Answer at the end of the chapter)

Many people are familiar with the rhyme about counting magpies:

One for sorrow
Two for joy
Three for a girl and
Four for a boy
Five for silver
Six for gold
Seven for a secret

Never to be told
Eight for a wish and
Nine for a kiss
Ten a surprise you should not miss
Eleven for health
Twelve for wealth
Thirteen beware it's the Devil himself.

The convention is to count the number of individual birds in a flock as a kind of prophecy or fortune-telling. Three birds, then, would point to the future birth of a baby girl, and five birds would mean that the observer is about to come into some money. In practice, with this version of the rhyme, nothing untoward is likely to be predicted, because, magpies being particularly sociable birds (they really do flock together), 'one for sorrow' is never likely to happen, or at least a magpie that appears to be solitary will almost certainly have companions nearby. If it becomes necessary, though, a handy tip to avert the sorrow, taught to me by my neighbour in Walsall, is to bow to the single magpie and say 'Good morning (or afternoon) Mr Magpie.' It always seems to work. A flock of thirteen would be unusually large, so a meeting with the Devil is only a remote possibility. That said, however, a few years ago a correspondent in an RSPB chat room asked, with reference to the rhyme, what fourteen magpies meant, as he had counted that number in one tree in his garden. He received the responses, 'I think it means you have a lot of magpies!' and 'Fourteen is two secrets never to be told!'

Recently I came across another version of the rhyme collected from Birmingham teenagers. It's rather more earthy than the more well-known one:

> One for anger
> Two for mirth
> Three for a wedding
> Four for a birth
> Five for rich and
> Six for poor
> Seven for a bitch and
> Eight for a whore
> Nine for a burying
> Ten for a dance
> Eleven for England and
> Twelve for France.

In 1486 *The Book of Saint Albans* was published (or *Boke of Seynt Albans*); it dealt with matters 'of interest to gentlemen'. In the category of 'Hunting', it listed collective nouns for a number of animals and birds, known as 'terms of venery', venery being the word current at the time for hunting. It is from this book that many of our colourful and extravagant collective nouns for birds originate, though many more have been added and invented as the centuries passed.

The terms of venery for magpies are: charm, congregation, flock, gulp, mischief, murder, tiding, tittering and tribe. Mischief, tittering and tribe seem particularly apposite to the character of these birds; flock is perhaps understated; congregation is somewhat literal; charm and tiding are poetic; but murder?

Magpies are, of course, members of the crow family, or corvids, and 'murder' as a collective noun is most often applied to carrion crows, although they are usually solitary birds, and hooded crows. The reasons for the term lie in folklore and a rather chilling little folktale. Some believe that it is simply the crows' black plumage that is associated with death, and by extension, murder. Others note that many in the crow family, particularly ravens and carrion crows, are scavengers and are attracted to decaying flesh, so in past centuries they have been seen to feed in battlefields and on gibbet-hung corpses; and there is an old belief that crows will circle over the spot where a death is to occur.

Here is the folktale.

A MURDER OF CROWS

The modern Michaelmas Day is the 29th of September, but this story concerns Old Michaelmas, the 10th of October. This is the day on which Lucifer was thrown out of heaven and his fall to earth was broken by a blackberry bush. Far from being grateful for this prickly cushion, the fallen angel cursed the poor blackberry, and in a belt and braces approach to destroying the fruit, he is believed to have spat on it, stamped on it and scorched it with his breath. So it is said that the blackberry is unfit to be eaten after this date.

Old Michaelmas was also one of the 'quarter days' of the year, when servants might be hired, rents were due and the harvest of the summer's crops should be complete. It was the start of autumn and the shortening of days, with colder weather ahead and long dark nights to be borne.

On a farm nestled amongst the gently sloping hills and valleys in the heart England some of the poorest people had gathered following the harvest, walking the field and patiently picking up fallen grains of corn one by one – and so had the crows. Sensing, as wild creatures do, the coming of the harsher weather, they, too, searched amongst the stubble to find whatever food they could.

The field was large, bordered by hedges of hawthorn, blackthorn and holly, with occasional mature trees, oak and ash and elm, hundreds of years old, some almost as old as the farm on which they grew. Though dwarfed by the trees, the hedgerow proudly displayed the exuberant growth put on throughout the long spring and summer days, awaiting the quieter times of early winter when the workers would come with their axes, cutting almost through the sturdy stems and plashing them towards the ground so that new, dense growth would start up at the turn of the year. Some of the poor folk would help with this work, rewarded with bundles of the trimmed branches to burn in their hearths at home. But for now, long bramble stems snaked and arched over and through the hedge, bearing fruit as black and shiny as a crow's back, dull red berries and a scattering of late flowers like pale pink stars, and the gleaners, both human and crow, went over to the hedge from time to time to refresh themselves with the sweet, dark blackberries.

Perhaps it was a mistake to eat fruit that had been cursed and spoiled by Lucifer himself, or perhaps it was simply the desperation of hunger that made the folk act in the way they later did; and the crows, what of them? Were they drawn into the Dark One's web of evil, or were they simply driven by their wild and primitive nature?

Whatever the cause, this is what happened. The people in the field had been there since first light, and although as the hours passed their pockets were filling with grain, it would be little enough to sustain them over the coming days. The crows had flown in at dawn as well, filling their crops with food enough for a day, perhaps two. One of the people looked up, her eye caught by a movement on the far side of the field. There was a stranger, and how he had got in was anyone's guess – there was no gate over there, and the hedge was dense enough to keep out any but the most determined. The woman whispered to her nearest companion, who, with his hands easing his aching back, slowly straightened up, gazed across the bare ground at the lone figure then passed on the message, until all of those poor folk had stopped their work and were watching the intruder.

The crows, a safe distance from the humans, lifted their heads as one and fixed their gaze on another newcomer. A bird, black like themselves but not of themselves, not known to them. As if in response to some invisible signal, they all took flight, swooped across the field and clustered in the topmost branches of the silent elm.

The people edged closer to one another, forming a tense knot. Few words were spoken. The gleaning rights on this land were theirs. They all knew hunger, they all knew fear. Many of them had starving children. Some of them had ageing parents. Some carried sticks, some had nailed boots, they all had fists. Together they moved across the rough ground, some striding, others trailing behind.

The elm twigs seemed too slender to support the weight of the heavy birds. The crows bobbed and swayed in the fresh breeze, cawing and calling one to another, loud, urgent. At once, wings spread, close enough almost to touch, they dropped from the tree, then letting the air carry them up, circled twice before sweeping down upon their victim.

The stranger sensed their approach before he heard it. He stared at the mob for only a moment, and ran, his eyes darting to and fro, searching for the weak place in the hedge where he had forced his way through. Long legged, he outran his pursuers, but where was it? He reached the boundary and dashed along it, haste was everything, seeking, not finding. He was dimly aware of the gang changing direction to head him off, closer, ever closer, and there it was, a gap in the hedge. He flung himself to the ground, dragging along on knees and elbows, almost through – when a spiny rope of bramble caught him around the waist. He struggled and kicked even as he felt hands closing on his legs and ankles, hauling him back.

The lone crow had seen the flock flying to their parliament in the tree. She had heard their crescendo of cries, she had watched as they wheeled in the sky. As they descended upon her she took to her wings, first rising then keeping the straight course for which her kind are famed, staying always ahead of her persecutors. They followed her until she was away from the land they called their own, then they turned away and flew back to the field.

A murder of crows. So-called because crows are believed to plot together to cause a death.

To end this chapter, a rather lighter story.

THE SEVEN BIRDS

An old couple were out on a bicycle ride one sunny afternoon. They found themselves cycling along the Hagley Road West in Smethwick, and they saw ahead of them the Cock and Magpies pub. Feeling a little thirsty and ready for a break, they pedalled into the car park and went inside. To their embarrassment, it was only when they were standing at the bar when they realised that neither of them had remembered to bring any money.

They asked the landlady if she could possibly put it on the slate, and they would promise to come back the next day and pay. The landlady considered this proposal, then she said, 'Well I would, but I can't give any credit until the landlord of the Queslett in Sutton gives me back the bottle of whisky he borrowed from me. If you get me the whisky, I can give you a drink.'

So the old couple got back on their bikes and they rode all the way to the Queslett. They went in and spoke to the landlord: 'Could we have the whisky that you owe the landlady at the Cock and Magpies so that she can give us a drink please?'

The landlord considered this proposal, then he said, 'Well I would, but I can't spare the whisky until the landlady of the Fox and Goose in Washwood Heath gives me back the bottle of rum she borrowed from me. If you get me the rum, I can give you the whisky.'

So the old couple, seeing a bit
of a jaunt ahead of them, left
their bikes at the Queslett
and caught the X4 bus
and the number 28 to
the Fox and Goose. They
went in and spoke to the
landlady: 'Could we have
the rum that you owe the
landlord of the Queslett so
that he can give us the whisky
that he owes the landlady of the
Cock and Magpies so that she can give
us a drink please?'

The landlady considered this proposal, then she said, 'Well I
would, but I can't spare the rum until the landlord of the Firebird
in Edgbaston gives me back the bag of cheesy nibbles that he owes
me. If you get me the cheesy nibbles, I can give you the rum.'

So the old couple wondered for a moment how they were going
to get to the Firebird, when a man in the corner piped up. 'I'm
going to the Firebird, I'll give you a lift.' The couple gratefully
accepted Derek's offer, and off they went to the Firebird. They went
in and spoke to the landlord: 'Could we have the bag of cheesy
nibbles that you owe the landlady of the Fox and Goose, so that
she can give us the rum that she owes the landlord of the Queslett
so that he can give us the whisky that he owes the landlady of the
Cock and Magpies so that she can give us a drink please?'

The landlord considered this proposal, then he said, 'Well I
would, but I can't spare the cheesy nibbles until the landlady of the

Goose at Kings Heath gives me back the bottle of slimline tonic she owes me. If you get me the slimline tonic, I can give you the cheesy nibbles.'

Because this is a story, there was a tram from Edgbaston to Kings Heath, so off the old couple went on the tram to the Goose. They went in and spoke to the landlady: 'Could we have the bottle of slimline tonic that you owe the landlord of the Firebird, so he can give us the bag of cheesy nibbles that he owes the landlady of the Fox and Goose, so that she can give us the rum that she owes the landlord of the Queslett so that he can give us the whisky that he owes the landlady of the Cock and Magpies so that she can give us a drink please?'

The landlady considered this proposal, then she said, 'Well I would, but I can't spare the slimline tonic until the landlord of the Swan at Yardley gives me back the box of dishwasher tablets he owes me. If you get me the dishwasher tablets, I can give you the bottle of slimline tonic.'

So the old couple looked on the map and saw that Yardley was only five and a half miles away and part of the route was Fox Hollies Road. With a name like that it was obviously a country park or something like that, and they decided to walk. They eventually arrived at the Swan having seen few hollies and no foxes. They went into the Swan and spoke to the landlord: 'Could we have the box of dishwasher tablets that you owe the landlady at the Goose so she can give us the bottle of slimline tonic that she owes the landlord of the Firebird, so he can give us the bag of cheesy nibbles that he owes the landlady of the Fox and Goose, so that she can give us the rum that she owes the landlord of the Queslett so that he can give us the whisky that he owes the landlady of the Cock and Magpies so that she can give us a drink please?'

The landlord considered this proposal, then he said, 'Well I would, but I can't spare the box of dishwasher tablets until the landlady of the Swallow in Solihull gives me back the six quid she owes me. If you get me the six quid, I can give you the box of dishwasher tablets.'

So the couple got on the X2 bus to the Swallow. They went in and spoke to the landlady: 'Could we have the six quid you owe the landlord of the Swan so he can give us the box of dishwasher tablets he owes the landlady at the Goose so she can give us the bottle of slimline tonic that she owes the landlord of the Firebird, so he can give us the bag of cheesy nibbles that he owes the landlady of the Fox and Goose, so that she can give us the rum that she owes the landlord of the Queslett so that he can give us the whisky that he owes the landlady of the Cock and Magpies so that she can give us a drink please?'

The landlady considered this proposal, then she said, 'Sounds reasonable, here you are.' And she gave them the six quid.

Back on the X2 bus to Yardley, into the Swan, the couple gave the six quid to the landlord. He gave them the box of dishwasher tablets. In a triumph of hope over experience, they again walked the five-and-a-bit miles to the Goose at Kings Heath. The walk was no better on the way back, but they did receive a bottle of slimline tonic from the landlady in exchange for the dishwasher tablets. Now the non-existent tram to Edgbaston, into the Firebird with the slimline tonic, where the landlord gave them a reciprocal bag of cheesy nibbles which were duly transported to the Fox and Goose in Washwood Heath once Derek had been cajoled into taking them in his car. The landlady of the Fox and Goose handed over the bottle of rum and the old couple nursed it carefully on the number 28 bus and the X2, to hand it over the bar of the Queslett in Sutton Coldfield. Bikes retrieved, now the final leg of the journey with the whisky from the Queslett's landlord to the Cock and Magpies in Hagley Road West, where the landlady took possession of the proffered bottle and called time.

Riddle answer: A magpie.

And finally, one more collective noun for crows, rooks or ravens: a storytelling.

6

GUNS AND EDWARD WOOLLEY

North of St Chad's Queensway in Birmingham are a few well preserved buildings, the remnants of the once-thriving gun manufacturing industry for which the city was famous. Until the 1960s, there were many more of the old factories still standing, but a swathe of the historic premises was demolished to allow for the building of the inner ring road, of which St Chad's Queensway is a part. The area was, and still is, known as the 'Gun Quarter'. The city council caused an outcry in 2011 when, in an attempt to distance itself from gun crime, it proposed renaming the area St George's and St Chad's Quarter. The plan was dropped, and The Gun Quarter remains.

Small arms manufacture suited the geography of the town. Twenty miles from a sizeable river, about as far as you can get from the sea in England and built on a plateau, Birmingham could not import and export weighty goods. The town relied on its canals and before that its turnpikes. The swords and guns produced were lighter, and therefore easily transported.

The next story features guns, and quality guns at that. The gun maker's art is a complex one, with many skilled workers combining their efforts. A barrel might be made from a sheet of steel that the craftsman passes between two rollers, one convex and one concave, to roll it into a tube.

The high quality Damascus barrels are made differently, and have a beautiful, unmistakeable finish. Alternate layers of red-hot iron and steel at white heat are twisted together, then coiled round a bar, reheated and welded into a barrel shape. When finished and polished, the barrels look rather as if they are watermarked with regular, subtle, swirling patterns.

Another worker would make the stock; a costly gun might well use French or Italian walnut, shaped and painstakingly polished to show the distinctive grain and colour.

The lock and other mountings may be made in Birmingham, or in a number of the surrounding towns. The separate pieces were often polished by women workers before the final assembly and then the engraving was completed by another specialist artisan. The whole, if we ignore its purpose, was a work of art and an example of skilled craft.

EDWARD WOOLLEY

If today you drive on the Black Country Route through Bilston, you will pass a Morrison's superstore. It's nice enough, as supermarkets go, but it's the site itself that is interesting – at least, for the purposes of this story. It was previously occupied for more than a century by Joseph Sankey and Son, manufacturers of many of the iron and steel products for which the West Midlands is renowned: screws, lockers, office furniture, radiators, hollow ware, pressed steel trays, steel wheels, frames and axles, culinary utensils and much more; it seems that virtually everything that could be made from iron or steel was made at some point at Sankey's.

Not so for the owner of the site before Joseph Sankey took it over. Edward Woolley was a well-known character in old Bilston. Referred to locally as 'Screw 'Oolley', he owned and ran a screw factory in what was then Albert Street. It seems that the business was reasonably profitable, or at least it provided Woolley with an income sufficient to live in a house grand enough to be called 'Oolley's Hall', which was approached through an avenue of trees.

But although Edward Woolley provided employment for forty men, and himself believed he should be afforded respect both as a local dignitary and as a former member of the Staffordshire Yeomanry (albeit briefly), it seems that the populace of Bilston did not altogether agree.

In short, he was seen as pompous and self-regarding. He would take it upon himself to issue instructions to the night-watchmen of the town, to the parish constable, and even to the constable's superiors, whilst the area magistrate (who might understandably have had an opinion in those matters) took no such liberties.

Woolley drew attention to himself further by affecting a style of dress which was, even in those times, bizarrely old-fashioned: shoes with prominent silver buckles, silk stockings and knee-breeches. He thought it gave him the air of a gentleman of the old school, but unfortunately this impression (if it was ever created in the first place) was destroyed as soon as he opened his mouth. As we have seen in a previous chapter, he habitually and publicly swore fit to make a trooper blush, while appearing to be enjoying himself hugely.

He was a small man, at least in height if not in girth, and he was a frequent sight on the streets of Bilston: driving in his low, old-fashioned carriage, often stopping to offer his opinion in his piercingly squeaky voice on any matter at all, provided it did not concern him in the least, while gesturing extravagantly with his whip.

Although it is clear that Edward Woolley had enough sense to own and successfully run a factory, even there the strangeness of his ways were apparent. Every day, he would carry from his home to the factory a little gift for the chief engineer – a parcel of fat from the previous night's joint. Woolley would present it to the man with the words 'Put that on your journals, it will make the wheels fly round.' He also had an abiding fear of a boiler explosion, and he was continually instructing his workers to lessen the steam pressure, 'Or you'll blow the place up!'

WHAT'S O'CLOCK, MR WOOLLEY?

One evening, Woolley was drinking in the front parlour of the Bull's Head in the High Street with several of his cronies. They smoked their long clay pipes and talked of this and that, while each man took his turn to order more ale for the company. So it was that, with the evening only half gone, the atmosphere amongst the occupants of the parlour was already jocular, loud and – as we shall see – a little rash.

As a servant was passing amongst the company with a large brown saltware jug, refilling yet again each man's flagon, a stranger entered. He was tall, of upright bearing and he wore a military greatcoat. He was followed closely by his servant, dragging a leather trunk. The tall man, with a polite but reserved nod to the friends, called for the landlord in a lilting Irish accent. Woolley and his companions looked at one another and exchanged smiles, but no-one spoke. The Irish officer, for that is what he was, requested a room for the night; the landlord led him up a flight of stairs that rose directly out of the parlour, the servant with the travelling trunk bringing up the rear.

Here was something out of the ordinary, and an opportunity for Woolley and company to create a little entertainment for themselves.

'I wonder,' said Woolley to no-one in particular, 'if the Irish can tell the time by an English watch?'

Several voices chorused: 'I've heard the answer's no!'

'Are you going to find out, Woolley?'

'I'll put money on it, what do you say?'

'We all know the Irish aren't as clever as the English!'

And soon the wager was made: Woolley would not dare to ask the Irish gentleman officer if he could tell the time by Woolley's watch.

And so, Woolley had to dare.

He called for the inn's servant, whose first task was to circulate amongst the gentlemen with a plate, collecting their wager money. Woolley then unclipped his fob watch from its chain and gave it to the servant, with the instructions that he was to take it upstairs, offer it to the Irish officer and enquire whether he could tell the time. The servant, who unlike the assembled gentlemen had not been drinking, could immediately imagine several outcomes of that course of action, and none were good. But he was there to do as he was told, and moreover he was promised a share of the gathered monies, so he took the watch and started up the stairs. He returned empty-handed soon afterwards, shrugged to the company, and made himself scarce.

The room became very quiet. Some of the men began to wonder if it had been such a good idea – but then, it wasn't their watch. After several minutes, they heard feet descending from the floor above, and they saw on the stairs the shoes, the legs and then the whole of the Irish officer's servant. He was carrying a silver tray, and he positioned himself in silence at the side of the room. Moments later, there was a heavier, more measured tread. A pair of highly polished riding boots came into view, then tailored breeches, a very fine fitted jacket, and finally the grimly unsmiling face of the officer.

He took his time scanning the room, looking at everyone in turn, who to a man avoided his gaze. He gestured for his servant to come forwards, and indicated the tray.

'You will see, gentlemen, that I have here a fine watch; and also you will see a brace of pistols. I invite the owner of the watch to step forward, claim it, and to make his choice of pistol.'

You hear of people who are drunk suddenly becoming sober when faced with a life-threatening challenge. This does not in fact happen; the drunk merely starts to wish fervently with a small part of his brain that he could sober up and think clearly, while the rest of his brain remains just as fogged and uselessly befuddled as before. But at least everyone in the room was able to scrape together enough good sense to keep quiet.

The officer raised an eyebrow. 'No one? Come now, gentlemen, you cannot have forgotten so soon whose watch this is. Perhaps you need a closer look.' He gestured his servant forward, who progressed slowly around the room, offering the tray to each man in turn. Each of them glanced at the watch and tried not to look too hard at the pistols, though none of them was so drunk that he did not recognise the quality. Woolley was aware of the servant approaching ever nearer, and finally the tray was there in front of his nose. Without so much as glancing at the tray's contents, he shook his head and turned away. The servant returned to his master, who said to him, 'Well now, it seems that you have gained a watch, so put it in your pocket. Go and pack up my things and bring the trunk down here.'

The servant returned to the upstairs room while the officer folded his arms and leaned against the wall, never taking his eyes from the company. After the most uncomfortable few minutes of their lives, they were inexpressibly relieved when they heard the servant's footsteps on the stairs, and the thump of the trunk descending behind him. When he was again at his master's side, the officer said, 'Saddle the horses, we will find another place to stay. The people here, it would seem, do not know how to welcome a stranger or how to treat a gentleman.' He turned and stalked from the room.

Who it was that told the tale of Edward Woolley's humiliation was never known. Perhaps it was one of Woolley's friends, perhaps it was the inn's servant. But word got around, and it was little more than a week later that Woolley was driving through the town and he heard, for the first time but not by any means the last, the call 'What's o'clock, Mr 'Oolley?'

THE PATIENT COACHMAN

Perhaps it would be as well to add a little anecdote that shows Edwards Woolley in a kinder light.

On his daytime excursions around the town, Edward Woolley used to drive a pony and trap, but on his evening outings to the Bull's Head, he travelled in a coach driven by his coachman.

Woolley entered the inn in search of company in the parlour, while the coachman gave the horse a nosebag, covered it with a rug, and then settled himself inside the coach with his pipe. After a decent interval, when he had finished a pipeful of tobacco, the coachman went into the inn and knocked on the parlour door. Woolley, with a wink to his friends, called 'Enter!' and the coachman came in.

'It's been a little while now, Mr Woolley, would you be wanting to go home?'

Edward Woolley, with an air of innocence, replied, 'No, that's all right Michael, I'm quite settled thank you.' The coachman had to return to the coach and empty pipe.

A little more time passed, and the coachman knocked again, was admitted and asked the same question. Edward Woolley looked about him as if considering his circumstances.

'No, thank you Michael, I seem to be very well provided for here.' The coachman withdrew once more.

When there was a third knock at the door, Edward smiled broadly at his companions before bidding the coachman to enter.

'Come along, Michael,' said Woolley, before the coachman had time to speak. 'We know what you really want, don't we? I'll stop my teasing now.' He called the inn servant and placed his order, and shortly, Michael the coachman was quite content, sitting with a pipeful of tobacco, a tankard and a large jug to fill it with, and a slice of pie and bread and cheese beside him.

THE YOUNG POACHER

One more story with a gun at its centre.

William was the name of the gamekeeper, and William was the name of his master, the Viscount Dudley. William was also the name of the king who, seven centuries before this story starts, left his home in Normandy to do battle with the English and, as the victor, laid claim to vast tracts of common land across the country as his own hunting grounds.

So the poor people who had relied on a little hunting to feed their families found that pursuit of the hart and the hind, the buck and the doe, pheasant and partridge, the hare and the coney, made them outlaws. But families have to be fed, and over hundreds of years poachers suffered the consequences when they were caught.

In the late 18th century, a young man named Ralph Bossock was the son of a family living in Prestwood Lane, Wall Heath. Even today, Wall Heath is a village; in those times, it was a tiny hamlet. The Bossocks had a small amount of land surrounding their cottage, and with a few animals they scraped a living of sorts. They were known to help themselves from time to time to the Viscount's game in nearby Himley Woods, but none of their neighbours would blame them for it – it was that or starve.

It was a dark and windy night when Ralph stood up from his seat by the cottage fire and took his old flintlock over his arm. His father held up a hand to stop him.

'Take care, son. You know what William Griffiths has done. Them man traps he's set are vicious, just like him.'

Ralph nodded. He knew, just like his father, of the stories that were going round; about how Griffiths had designed a man trap more powerful than any other, and had had a number of them made at the Wednesfield smithy. The cruel traps were hidden in undergrowth and were certain to mutilate anyone who stepped on one.

'I'll be careful, dad. I know my way around the woods.' With that, Ralph shouldered his game bag and was gone.

Later that night, one of the under-gamekeepers went to find William Griffiths in his lodge. He had found grisly evidence of poaching: one of the man-traps had sprung, its massive jagged-toothed jaws snapping together, and caught in the teeth was the lower part of a man's leg. Griffiths called for more of his men, ordering them to bring loaded guns, and the hunt was on. They gathered at the trap; it was as the first man had described it. Griffiths held his lantern close and examined it carefully.

'It looks as though he had to cut away his own leg to escape,' he said. The youngest of his men turned away and retched into the bushes. The faces of the others were grim as Griffiths pointed to the trail of blood.

It was easy to follow, even by lantern light, and it led them to Wall Heath and Prestwood Lane. They found Ralph Bossack cowering in the family pigsty. Deep in shock and having lost a lot of blood, he offered no resistance and was taken away.

The poacher survived and stood trial. There was no denying what he had been doing; his lower leg was even shown as evidence. If he expected any leniency from the judge because of what he had already suffered, then he was disappointed. He was sentenced to seven years' transportation to Australia, a sentence that could often mean death.

Ralph's father, Old Man Bossack, swore that he would have his revenge on William Griffiths, but ten years passed and no harm came to the gamekeeper.

Late in 1807 winter had taken hold and it was colder than it had been for years. Griffiths knew that in the bitter weather, and with Christmas approaching, the temptation to take game from the Viscount's woods would be greater than ever. He had men on watch all day and night in three shifts, and he himself would rise early every morning to conduct his own inspection. One morning, he did not return to his lodge at the expected time, and some of his men went in search of him. He was found in Holbeche Croft.

It was a horrific sight. He was lying in his own blood, his body slashed, his head crushed in one of his own man traps. It seemed to be an extremely brutal pointed message.

The local constable was called, and he found some tracks in the frozen snow that led to and from the body. There were footprints, but from only one boot; beside them were round holes in the snow, of a kind that could have been made by a peg-leg.

Everyone remembered what had happened to Ralph Bossack. The rumours flew from mouth to ear: Ralph had come back and killed his hated adversary. But when enquiries were made, it was found that he had died in Perth in 1801. Suspicion fell on Old Man Bossack, who had sworn vengeance all those years before, but no evidence was found against him, and eventually the constabulary dropped the investigations. The crime remained unsolved.

Over the following years, the Bossack family moved away from Wall Heath, all but Old Man Bossack, who stayed on in the dilapidated cottage until his death in 1827. The cottage remained empty, deteriorating year on year, until 1836 when it was demolished. The workman who was dismantling the fireplace and chimneybreast made a strange discovery. Inside the chimney on a hidden shelf was a peg leg. It was scorched and smoke-blackened, but still intact and there could be no mistaking what it was. Perhaps Old Man Bossack had, after all, wreaked the vengeance he had threatened. It is a secret he took with him to his grave.

7

AYNUK AND AYLI

A wise man once pointed out that not all stories are jokes, but all jokes are stories, and here are some little stories about Black Country favourites, Aynuk and Ayli. Aynuk and Ayli, or Enoch and Eli, have been the subject of much Black Country humour for decades, and they are sometimes quick-witted and cunning, sometimes slow and hapless: the archetypical wise fools. Some of their stories are jokes that you may have heard before, and many of their stories have a distinct Black Country flavour. If you would like to picture them it may help to know

that often, when they are drawn by cartoonists, both wear flat caps and shabby trousers and jackets; Aynuk is tall and thin while Ayli is short and chubby. When telling a set of Midlands tales, I find the occasional Aynuk and Ayli story can add variety and comic relief.

Aynuk got himself a new job, labouring on a building site near Cradley. The gaffer came by to see how he was getting on. Aynuk had laid three bricks.

'Aynuk,' he said, 'you're the slowest man on the site. Hurry up, can't you?'

The gaffer came by the next day and Aynuk had only laid another four bricks.

'Aynuk! If you don't work harder, I'm going to have to take it out of your wages!'

The next day the gaffer came by again, and Aynuk seemed to have slowed down even more, with just another two bricks added to the wall.

'Aynuk, you're the laziest man I've ever met! Nothing I say makes any difference to you. I just can't seem to get you to work!'

Aynuk smiled sympathetically. 'Well, gaffer, try not to mek yersel' feel bad about it. It ay (isn't) your fault. I cor (can't) mek mesel' work neither!'

A man is walking through the Black Country and he sees Aynuk and Ayli in the street, busily propping up a wall. He asks them how far it is to Bilston. Aynuk and Ayli look at each other, and debate for a few moments.

'Er, we think it's about seven mile,' says Aynuk, and Ayli chips in, 'But if yo' run, yo' might do it in five.'

Ayli gets a job on a farm. One day, he's taking a pile of muck along a lane in a cart, when the back of the cart, which he is supposed to have secured, flies open, and a large quantity of horse muck ends up in a pile on the road. Ayli grabs a shovel and starts frantically heaving the muck back into the cart, but such is the size of the heap, he's soon red in the face and sweating without having made much impression on it. At that moment, his friend Aynuk happens to pass by.

'Ayli! Why bist (are) thee workin' so hard?'

Ayli continues shovelling, panting with the exertion. 'I cor (can't) stop. The gaffer wo' like it!'

Aynuk tries again. 'Ayli! Yo'll gie yersel' a heart attack, workin' like that. Slow down, man!'

Ayli still works as fast as he can. 'I cor stop. The gaffer wo' like it!'

Aynuk plays his trump card. 'Come on, Ayli. There's the Frock and Feathers just aroun' the corner. What say thee to a pint o' ale?'

Ayli, redder than ever and streaming with sweat, says, 'I cor stop. The gaffer wo' like it!'

Aynuk is finally exasperated with his friend's unreasonableness. 'Ayli! The gaffer cor be that 'ard, surely? Where is the man? I'll gie 'im a piece o' my mind!'

Still shovelling, Ayli nods at the pile of manure. 'Under 'ere!'

One evening, when Aynuk and Ayli are supping a pint or two in the Frock and Feathers, they start reminiscing about their families.

'My granferther,' says Aynuk thoughtfully, 'in the First World War, singlehandedly destroyed the enemy's lines of communication.'

Ayli took a swig of his ale. 'Oh, aye. How did 'e do that, then, all on his own?'

Aynuk paused for effect. 'He et their pigeon!'

During the First World War, the man who later in life will become Aynuk's grandfather, is with his comrades in a trench, under bombardment from the enemy. For some time the platoon has been awaiting orders which will be delivered by carrier pigeon. At last, scanning the sky, Aynuk's grandfather sees a pigeon with what looks like a message attached to its leg, and he shouts out, 'There it is!'

But the fortunes of war are harsh, and no sooner has the bird been spotted than it falls from the air and lands 100 yards or so away, in the mud of no man's land.

The platoon commander decides that, as Aynuk's grandfather was the first to sight the bird, then he should be the one to venture out under enemy fire and retrieve the message. So he climbs over the top and scurries off in the rough direction of the bird's descent.

He is gone a long time, and his comrades begin to despair of him ever returning, but after an hour his cheery face appears, a lot dirtier, as he scrambles back into the trench. The men burst into spontaneous applause, and then give three cheers for their hero.

'Well?' asks the commander. 'Did you find it?'

'Oh, ar, I did, sir,' replies Aynuk's grandfather.

'And was there a message?'

'Oh, ar, there was, sir.'

The commander is losing patience. 'Well, what was it?'

'It said Cooooo, sir, Cooooo!'

Aynuk and Ayli had spent most of their dinner time in the Frock and Feathers. Emerging into the street, they decide that now they are no longer thirsty, they had better do something about their growing hunger. So they wander a few yards down the road, push through the swing door and approach the counter.

Without needing to ask Ayli, Aynuk reels off their usual order. 'One 'addock, love, one cod, mek it a big 'un, and two cones o' chips. Leave it open, plaise, we'll ate it now.'

The woman behind the counter eyes Aynuk coldly. 'This is the library.'

A little blearily, Ayli looks round the room, and takes in the shelves of books. 'Ay, Aynuk, her's right thee knows.' He turned to address the librarian.

'Sorry, love.' And he lowers his voice to a whisper: 'One 'addock, one cod, mek it a big 'un.'

I have come across many little stories which feature Aynuk's or Ayli's wives, but none unfortunately where they have a name. This one is no different.

It was Aynuk's wife's birthday, and he decided she would like to go to an air show, largely because he had won some free tickets in the Frock and Feathers' monthly raffle.

They have a pleasant enough day, viewing vintage aircraft and watching the Red Arrows display. Aynuk's wife says, 'I'd love to go up in a plane, Aynuk.'

In an uncharacteristic display of generosity, Aynuk, who had earlier noticed that the pilot of a light aircraft was offering trips in his plane, offers to pay for a flight for both of them. But when they stroll over to the plane in question, Aynuk sees that the flights cost £25 per person.

'That's far too much!' he says. 'I cor afford fifty pound!'

His wife is understandably annoyed, it after all being her birthday, and she protests in strong terms, whereupon they start to argue loudly.

The pilot, concerned that they will frighten off his potential customers, tries to intervene, but they take no notice. In the end, to shut them up, he offers to take them on a flight for half price, £25 for the two of them. Aynuk hastily agrees.

There is one condition that the pilot imposes, however: 'You two have to stop arguing. If I hear one peep out of either of you, you'll have to pay full price!'

They readily agree. They climb into the plane, and in very little time they are enjoying the most wonderful flight. The pilot decides to test their nerve, and their resolve to remain silent, and he performs every aerobatic trick he knows. He twists, rolls, dives, spins and finally loops the loop, several times. But there is no sound at all from his passengers.

When they are safely landed, he comments, 'I really thought one of you at least might say something when I was performing all those tricks. I've got to admit, you've got strong nerves!'

Aynuk's wife said, 'Well, I wondered if I should mention it when Aynuk fell out a while back, but I knew he'd say £25 is £25!'

Ayli walks into a shop and says, 'I'd like to buy a wasp plaise.'

The shopkeeper, a little bemused, says, 'I'm sorry, but we don't sell wasps.'

'Are yo sure?' asks Ayli. 'Yo've got three at least in the winder!'

Aynuk and Ayli are working on a building site, when they dig up an unexploded bomb.

'It must be from the war,' says Aynuk. 'We'd better put it in the barrer and tek it to the foreman later.'

So Aynuk and Ayli, with not a little difficulty, manage to hoist the bomb into the wheelbarrow, and they carry on digging.

A little later, what should they find but a second unexploded bomb. They decide to take it to the foreman in the same wheelbarrow, and they have just heaved it in when it rolls over and knocks against the first bomb. There is a click, a pause and then it starts ticking.

Aynuk is aghast. 'Oh no, Ayli, what are we gooin' ter do if this second bomb blows up?'

Ayli is sanguine. 'Doh worry, Aynuk, it doh matter. If it blows up, we'll just tell 'im we only found one.'

Aynuk and Ayli have got some casual work with the local council, digging holes in the park. A young woman with her toddler in a pushchair comes and sits on a bench opposite to where the men are working.

After watching them for half an hour or so, she is quite puzzled. Aynuk digs a hole, while Ayli leans on his spade and watches. Then Aynuk steps aside, and Ayli start to use his spade – to fill the hole back in. When Ayli has finished filling in the hole, he smacks the flat of his spade down onto the surface of the ground to flatten the earth, then the two of them shuffle along a few feet, and start the whole procedure again.

When Ayli has just finished filling in the third hole in a row, the young woman gets up and strolls over to them.

'I hope you don't mind me asking,' she says, 'but I couldn't help wondering what you were doing. One of you digs a hole, then the other one fills it in, then you start all over again. What's the point?'

Aynuk straightens up from digging the fourth hole. 'Well,' he says, 'usually, I dig a hole, Ed plants a tree in it, and Ayli fills it in.'

'But you haven't been planting any trees!' the young woman protests.

'That's because Ed's off sick. But it's not fair if we lose a day's pay because he's not here!'

Aynuk decided to do a bit of DIY, so he went along to the local hardware shop.

'I'd like some nails plaise,' he says.

'How long do you want them?' asks the assistant.

Aynuk pauses for thought. 'Well I was hoping to keep 'em.'

A journalist from London is making a documentary about the Black Country, and he is interviewing local characters.

It's Ayli's turn.

'So you live in the Black Country?' says the journalist.

'Ar, I do,' says Ayli.

'And have you lived here all your life?'

'Not yet,' says Ayli.

A journalist from London is making a documentary about the Black Country, and he is interviewing local characters.

It's Aynuk's turn.

'So you live in the Black Country?' says the journalist.

'Ar, I do,' says Aynuk.

'Which part?'

'All of me,' says Aynuk.

In their youth, Aynuk and Ayli were on the bus together. Ayli notices that Aynuk is holding a metal cylinder with a plastic cup on the top.

'What's that?' he asks.

'Oh, me mam gave it me. She says it's called a Thermos Flask.'

'A Thermos Flask?' says Ayli. 'What's that?'

'Well,' says Aynuk, 'me mam says it does two things. It can keep hot things hot and cold things cold.'

'That sounds amazin'. What have you got in it?'

'Two cups of tea and an ice lolly.'

Aynuk saves up and buys himself an old car. He's passed his test, but somehow the finer points of responsible driving have passed him by.

One evening, the local copper sees Aynuk come out of the Frock and Feathers. He weaves his way across the road and gets into his car. He starts it up and drives off, with the copper running in pursuit. Hearing the copper shouting, Aynuk brakes, coming to a halt in the middle of the road.

'What's going on, Bert?' says Aynuk, winding down the window as the man catches up with him.

'Aynuk, have you been drinking?'

'Ar, I 'ave. I bin to Ayli's and we had a few pints of his 'ome brew. Then I had to see a man about a dog in the Feathers, and I 'ad four pints o' mild, two or three pints o' best bitter and a small sherry.'

'Aynuk, I'm going to have to ask you to get out of the car and blow into this breathalyser.'

Aynuk looked hurt. 'What's the matter Bert?' he asked. 'Don't you believe me?'

Aynuk and Ayli are sitting in a café eating their packed lunches. The manager comes over.

'This is a café, not the local park. You can't eat your own food in here.'

Aynuk and Ayli say nothing, but swap sandwiches and carry on eating.

In the days when Aynuk and Ayli were working at the iron foundry, they got talking in one of their tea breaks about timekeeping.

Ayli expressed the opinion that he didn't need a watch. 'We've got one clock in the house, and it's in the kitchen. It's an owd one, but it strikes the hour.'

Aynuk was puzzled. 'So yo've got no watch, Ayli. Yo've only got the one clock, and it's in the kitchen. But yo'm never late for werk, and we start early. How do you do it?'

Ayli said it was easy, because he'd inherited his great uncle's bugle.

Aynuk was more puzzled. 'Yer great uncle's bugle? 'Ow does that 'elp yer know the time?'

Ayli said, 'When I wake up early in the mornin' an' I doh know what time it is, an' I haven't heard the kitchen clock chime, I get out of bed, open the winder and blow a few

blasts on me great uncle's bugle. Someone up the street's sure to throw open their winder and shout "Oo's blowin' a flamin' bugle at half past five in the mornin'?"'

Aynuk and Ayli decided to go on a cycling holiday together. They were worried about getting separated if one of them was faster than the other, so they hit on the plan of hiring a tandem.

Aynuk got on the front, and Ayli climbed on the back, and off they went towards Worcestershire, but it wasn't long before they came to a hill. They pedalled harder and harder, but they were making very slow progress. Ayli, red in the face and gasping for breath, managed to call out a few strangled words.

'It's 'ard, Aynuk, ay it? I dunno whether I con go much further.'

Aynuk tried to offer some encouragement.

'Keep goin' Ayli! I know it's a steep 'un, but I'm keepin' the brakes on so we doh slip back!'

Ayli ran into the Frock and Feathers, leaned on the bar and said to the landlord, 'Quick! Give me a pint o' mild afore the trouble starts.'

The landlord, with anxious glances towards the door, gave Ayli a pint of mild, which he downed in one. He banged the glass down on the bar, and said, 'Quick! Give me another, the trouble will be startin' soon!'

The landlord pulled another pint and gave it to Ayli, which he drank a little more slowly, but still soon finished.

'What trouble, Ayli?' asked the landlord. 'Do I need to lock the door?'

'I'll tell yo' in a minute,' said Ayli. 'Just give me one more a fore it starts.'

So the landlord gave him one more pint. 'Now come on, Ayli,' said the landlord. 'Tell me about this trouble that's going to happen.'

Ayli was careful to finish his drink before answering.

'It's like this: I got no money!'

Aynuk and Ayli went to a café for dinner. Aynuk was reading the menu from a chalkboard on the wall.

'Soup of the day,' he said. 'I wonder what that's like, Ayli?'

Ayli brightened up. 'Oh, ar, we should 'ave that. I went on a day out to Coventry with the missus yesterday, and we 'ad soup of the day and it wuz great!'

Ayli was sitting on the garden wall, watching Aynuk trooping back and forth to the garden shed, first taking in planks of wood, then pram wheels, then a toolbox, then assorted nails and screws. He went in and shut the door.

Ayli sat in the sun, listening to the sounds of sawing and hammering coming from Aynuk's shed. Eventually he got off the wall and strolled over to see what was going on. Ayli opened the door and peered in. Aynuk was squeezed up against the shed wall, trying to fix a wheel on a huge wooden box.

'What yo' doin', Aynuk?' asked Ayli.

'What does it look like? I'm mekkin' a handcart.'

'It looks amazin', Aynuk,' said Ayli, 'but 'ow yo' goin' ter get it outta the shed? It's bigger than the door.'

Aynuk's face clouded, then a thought occurred to him. 'I con tek it apart, cor I?'

Ayli was planning to make a cabinet for the kitchen, and knowing that Aynuk was an experienced carpenter, he went to ask his advice.

'How do I know whether to use a nail or use a screw, Aynuk?' asked Ayli.

'Well, I do it like this,' said Aynuk. 'I knock in a nail, and if the wood splits, then I know I shoulda used a screw.'

Aynuk and Ayli were on their tea break, and Aynuk was reading the paper. He suddenly looked at Ayli over the top of the paper.

'Some people say that if you're from the Black Country yo'm thick, doh they?'

'Ar, I believe so. That's what some people say,' said Ayli.

'Well, it ay true! It says 'ere that the population of London is the densest in the country!'

8

THE BLOXWICH BULL

Although now part of Walsall Metropolitan Borough, the town of Bloxwich is an ancient one. The Bull's Head pub, in Park Road, found its origins over five centuries ago; the name may have come from the bull's head which is part of the coat of arms of the Skeffington family, who owned land in and around the Bloxwich area in the sixteenth century. On the other hand, many pubs of this name are thus called after the cruel practice of bull-baiting, and unfortunately this was a popular 'sport' in the area for a long time.

It is recorded by the pub's last landlord that the Tudor grate in the fireplace was only removed in the late nineteenth century – presumably it wore out – and the original oak beams and inglenook fireplace were preserved. The Bull's Head was demolished in 1927 by Walsall Council, but the legend of its wishing tree remains. There is a photograph of the pub taken in 1927 by local historian Billy Meikle, and the wishing tree can be clearly seen not 20 feet away. By the patchwork effect of the bark, and the sycamore-like leaves, it seems to be a plane tree.

THE BLOXWICH WISHING TREE

Margaret Moseley was married to a miner. Now, miners at the time of this story, which is set around the end of the nineteenth century, used to work shifts; some might start at six in the morning and some might start in the afternoon. For those who were so inclined, there could be plenty of time in the day for drinking, and it seems that Margaret's husband Samuel was one who was so inclined.

There were times when mining was one of the better paid occupations, but as Margaret knew only too well, no matter how good wages are, they cannot be spent twice, and if a man is spending money in the pub for several hours every day, then it can leave a family short. She would have the worry, too, that each time he went to work down the mine after he had been drinking, he would be more likely to have an accident and injure himself and maybe injure some other woman's husband, too. Injury meant no work. No work meant no money.

On the day of this story, Samuel has risen late. No harm in that; he had been working late into the small hours. But no sooner was he up and dressed than he was out of the door and walking up the road to The Bull's Head. Margaret stayed at home as usual, taking care of the household tasks and preparing their dinner. Then the dinner was ready; then the dinner began to get cold, and still Samuel did not appear. Margaret sat for a while at the kitchen table, tapping her foot. She waited as long as she could, but the clock kept on ticking, and Margaret knew that Samuel's shift would be starting soon.

She stood up, her lips pressed into a thin line, and left the house, following the route her husband had taken two hours before. Into The Bull's Head she went, to find Samuel settled by the fire with a pint pot by his side. He blinked vaguely at his wife and attempted a smile. Margaret was not to be appeased. She put her hands on her hips.

'Your dinner's cold, you're supposed to be at work in half an hour, and you sit there drinking!'

Samuel opened his mouth to answer, but he could think of nothing to say. Just at that moment, two colliers came in from outside. They greeted Samuel by name, then turned and looked blankly at Margaret. In those days, in that pub, it was not the done thing for a man to be accompanied by his wife. Samuel returned their greeting, and his cheeks coloured. He cleared his throat and asked his colleagues to excuse him while he finished his conversation with his wife. He straightened his back and puffed out his chest.

'And another thing, Margaret, I'm the man of the house and I'll do what I want. In fact,' he tried to see out of the corner of his eye if the two other men were looking impressed, 'in fact, I don't think I feel like going to work at all today. No, I don't think I'll go.'

Margaret knew she would get no change out of him, not when he'd been drinking and not in front of his workmates. She hesitated for a few moments, then, afraid of making a fool of herself, strode out of the door before the tears came. Outside, she turned to face the pub. Wiping her eyes with a corner of her apron, she choked out the words, 'Curse you Samuel Moseley and curse the day I married you! I hope that damn pub falls on you and buries you!'

She started for home, but had only gone a few paces when her feelings got the better of her and she repeated the curse, standing under the plane tree. The words were barely out of her mouth when there was a creaking, a screeching of twisting wood and a resounding rumble of falling masonry. Margaret stared, horrified, as the pub's roof caved in, then she turned and fled, running and running until she was home, where she collapsed and fainted.

Samuel and his friends, all pitmen, were used to being alert to danger and the sounds of an imminent collapse. They only had to hear the first few groans from above their heads before they bolted for the door, just in time to see Margaret's flight. They stood a safe distance away, watching the pub's other occupants emerging with shocked and frightened faces.

In the event, not only did the pub not fall on Samuel Moseley and bury him, but it was just the roof that collapsed, damaging rooms and furniture in the upper floor, but leaving the ground floor untouched and all the human occupants unharmed. Nevertheless, the plane tree under which Margaret Moseley repeated her curse became known as The Wishing Tree, and many a resident of Bloxwich has stood under its branches to test its powers. The lovelorn, the hopeful, the desperate – all have put their faith in a simple tree.

Although the old Bull's Head was demolished in 1927, another pub with the same name was built by two women owners in 1928. The tree remained until the 1960s when, with a disregard for local history and legend, it was cut down so that a small car park could be built in front of the pub. The rebuilt pub fell into disrepair in the twenty-first century, and recently a block of flats were built on its site. How times change.

Today, at the far end of the High Street from the site of The Bull's Head is Elmore Green. It's a grassed area bordered by trees, and on the green a monument to the history of Bloxwich was placed in 2007. Called The Bloxwich Tardis, it is indeed roughly the size and shape of a police phone box. It was cast from iron and steel, and on the top, coloured gold, is a tree. The Wishing Tree.

The following story is my version of an old song given to me by storyteller Paul Butler. I have combined it with a historical incident.

THREE MEN AND A BULL

> *Come friends and listen to my song*
> *You shall not find it dulle*
> *It is the strange and merry lay*
> *About ye Bloxwich Bull.*

The green was thronging with people. Everyone had the day off work: the miners, the chain-makers and the iron foundry workers were looking forward to a day in the sunlight; the bridle-, bit- and stirrup-makers were anticipating a day away from forge and file; the saddle-makers and the lock-makers were expecting a relaxing day away from the workbench.

All the usual attractions and amusements were there, to tempt the men, women and children of the village to part with their cash. Stalls with food and drink shared the space with simple games, but the main event was yet to take place. A stake had been driven deep into the ground so that a bull might be tethered for the popular diversion of bull-baiting. Men and women drank in the alehouse next to the stable where the bull was kept under the watch of three men of the town; Amos, Bart and George had been taking turns for days to guard the valuable beast. Other men strutted about the green led by muscular and wild-eyed dogs on ropes. A lot of money would change hands that day; the dogs might be injured or killed by the bull, the bull would suffer attacks from the dogs, but the people would make money.

The time was approaching for the bull to be tied to the stake. The villagers began to drift towards the bull ring, some with tankards in hand, some chewing on beef sausages bought from a stall, all desirous of getting a good view. George was guarding the stable, and Amos and Bart approached across the green so all three might lead the bull to its fate.

George took the key from his pocket as the other two joined him, and he unlocked the Bloxwich-made padlock on the stable door. Pulling back the hasp, he began to swing the door open. A bull is a large animal; it was not an enormous stable. It was instantly clear, therefore, that the bull was not there, but nevertheless, the three hurried inside and looked around them, mouths open, as if their disbelief at the bull's absence could make it appear.

Amos was the first to speak. 'It's not 'ere!' he cried, somewhat unnecessarily.

Bart joined in. 'No, it ay. An' George was the last to watch it. Where's it gone, George?'

'I doh know! It wor my fault! You two bin watchin' it too, maybe it were gone 'afore my shift.' Amos and Bart considered that uncomfortable truth.

All three men pondered the possibility of accusing one or both of the others of being asleep on the nightshift, and each of them privately rejected the idea. All had in fact slept on their night watch, but none of them knew that the other two were as guilty as he.

Bart had an idea. 'Why doh we say it were the lock that failed?'

'Don't be stupid, Bart,' was Amos's scornful response. 'It were made at the locksmith's round the corner. If we try and pretend it were the lock's fault, we'd get strung up.'

Bart had to agree with the truth of Amos's assertion. The lock had one key which was kept by each man as he took up his watch. It could only be opened with the key, and no Bloxwich lock would open any other way.

'What to do then?' asked George, but none of them had an answer.

Just at that moment, there was a shout from the centre of the green. 'Come on, where is it? Bring it over 'ere, we've bin waitin' long enough!'

It was too late for the three to make their escape. Dog owners and a random assortment of men and women from the village were making their way towards the stable, faces eager. It was only a matter of a few moments before they arrived.

'Let's see it then,' said the first, a broad man with the florid complexion of a habitual drinker. He pushed past the three men, and stopped dead. 'What's gooin' on?' he demanded, as others clustered round and jostled to see into the stable.

Amos, Bart and George had no explanation, even though they each tried hard to put the blame on the other two. The people grabbed a firm hold of them and they were dragged to the bull ring. The broad florid man seemed to have appointed himself spokesman.

'Well, we've got no bull, it seems. No bull, nothing to bet on. So I say, we better tie you three to the stake, and let the dogs loose on you. I doh mind if I bet on a bull or a man!' The crowd cheered its assent.

The three men were shaking visibly. What had seemed like good sport when it was an animal who was suffering, now seemed horrific, a terrifying ordeal.

Amos found his voice and pleaded with the crowd to let them search for the bull. It couldn't be far away, he reasoned, and it wouldn't take them above an hour to find it. Surely they would give the three an hour's grace?

The people muttered amongst themselves and eventually the broad man spoke again. 'One hour. That's all. If you doh bring it within an hour, we'll know you've sold it, and we'll mek you pay!'

The three scurried away and began a search of all the stables and outbuildings of the village.

On the edge of the green, an old woman had been watching the events unfold. She had walked some miles to be there. Her name was Nanny Throttlecat, but in spite of that, she was an animal lover. The previous evening, she had called on one of the tradesmen of the town. She knew he was the right one; she had her methods. She gave him a twist of paper. The man thanked her and, as she walked away, wondered how she knew what had been in his mind.

Later that night the man had made his way to the stable, where he found Amos sitting on the ground with his back to the wall. The tradesman produced a bottle and offered to share it. Amos thought himself very cunning. When it was his turn to drink, he pretended to be taking a small sip, while actually sucking a large quantity of the liquid. The man did the opposite, having not long before added to the bottle Nanny Throttlecat's powder from the twist of paper.

When Amos woke up, he remembered nothing of the episode. Nor did he remember an old woman taking a key from his pocket and returning it a minute or two later.

The hour was up. The three men had disappeared, and the bull was still conspicuous by its absence. The villagers began to look for all four of them.

> *They searched from noon to twilight grey*
> *And then to evening dull*
> *But never more ye people spied*
> *Ye tall men or ye bull.*

THE DARLASTON BULL CLUB

The men of the Darlaston Bull Club liked to do things properly. They had formed themselves into a formally constituted organisation with a chairman and a treasurer. They met every week in the bar of the Black Horse in Pinfold Street, and while the meetings were largely of a social nature, they also included the serious business of collecting contributions from the members. The treasurer diligently noted down the sums in a ledger and issued receipts, continuing this practice week after week until the long-awaited day came when the chairman stood to make his announcement. He cleared his throat and glanced down at the notes he held in both hands. The club members fell silent, the air of anticipation palpable.

'Gentlemen,' said the chairman. 'I have received a report from our esteemed treasurer, and I am pleased to be able to announce that the Darlaston Bull Club is now in possession of sufficient funds to purchase three bulls and furthermore to rent the fields to keep them in.'

The news prompted a cheer and applause from the club members. The plans were rapidly concluded, with four members being entrusted with taking part of the money to the next cattle market to buy the bulls.

It was all going so well. The bulls were bought and installed in the fields of a farm on the northern side of the town. The club members now had a new topic of discussion: where could the bulls be taken to be baited, to start making the men's money back for them.

The following week, however, brought some shocking news. One club member, charged with the responsibility of making a daily check on the animals, reported, white-faced, that he had found that day not three but two bulls. Much discussion ensued, and the upshot was that the club members decided that it must be a gang from Willenhall, as the field was not 2 miles from the rival town. The club's investment must be protected, and this would be done by watching the fields. The treasurer wasted no time in drawing up a rota, with two men watching each night.

The watch started straight away, that very night. A chain and padlock secured the gate of each field, and two club members settled themselves under a hedge. Well, the day had been a long one, and the evening in the Black Horse had been convivial, and it was not long before both men were snoring. They woke at dawn, cold and cramped, to find that another bull had gone.

The club held an emergency meeting and it was decided by a unanimous vote that the important thing was to discover how the bulls were being removed from the field; clearly if the gate remained padlocked, the bulls must have been driven through the hedge, but where? The member who owned a paint shop proposed a solution; if the hedge was whitewashed, then it would be clear which part of the hedge was disturbed, so the bull would be easier to follow and the culprits could be brought to justice.

All that day, the club worked in the field with buckets of whitewash and brushes, watched with mild interest by the bull, and by the evening the hedges were all painted. Two men took up the watch, and the rest went home. This time, they were careful to stay awake, and they had indeed remained conscious for a good twenty minutes when they felt the first drops of rain. Moment by moment the rain grew heavier and soon there was a downpour. The watchmen scrambled to their feet and ran for the nearest cover, which happened to be the pub. They stayed there for the rest of the evening, gently steaming in front of the fire.

The next morning the two men went back to check on the bull. They found no bull, and with the rain cleaning the hedge of all the whitewash, they couldn't find the field, either. So that was the end of the Darlaston Bull Club.

Who had taken the bulls? That was never discovered, but we could guess.

9

WITCHES

Belief in witches persisted for centuries – indeed, there are still witches' covens today. They were feared as enemies and as having evil power granted to them by the Devil in return for their service to him, body and soul. Some were thought to be shapeshifters, commonly turning into hares or cats to carry out their sinister purposes.

Whether those who were identified as witches were indeed in league with the Devil is another matter. When times are hard, it must be tempting to look for someone to blame if the cow runs dry, or the crops fail, or the baby is ill.

It was largely, though by no means exclusively, women who were accused of witchcraft, and many lost their lives. A law was passed in England prohibiting the death penalty for witches in 1736, but the fear persisted. As late as 1875 a man, John Hayward, killed 80-year-old Ann Tennant, claiming that she had made his farm animals sicken and die by putting her 'evil eye' on them. So persuaded was Hayward that his victim was a witch, that he requested at his trial that her body be weighed against a Bible; the old belief was that a witch, regardless of his or her size, could not outweigh a Bible.

Not all witches were believed to be evil, though. Some people were accepted by their community as having special powers which they could be relied upon to use for good purposes. Perhaps they had a particular knowledge of herb lore and could help to heal and cure illness, the forerunners of today's herbalists. Many could offer simple charms to help with daily concerns: will it be a good harvest? Will the hens lay well? Does she/he love me?

Here are some stories that illustrate our abiding fascination with magic and those who know how to wield it.

OLD MOLLIE MOGG

The old turnpike road from Oldbury to Halesowen used to pass through Bleak Heath; it was well named, being miles of windswept and lonely heathland overlooked by the crouching presence of Powke Hillock.

The hillock was home to Mollie Mogg. Her house was built of the local hard dolerite, the Rowley Rag that had been quarried by the Romans; some said that Old Mollie remembered those times. But the hillock took her into its arms as its own; the land seemed to rise and fold around her hard stone cottage, weathered over centuries to the same colour as the tough grasses and heathers that grew on and around it. Bee orchids and hare's foot clover bloomed on the path to the door to be enjoyed by those who were able to find it.

Some did find the path. People came from Cradley Heath, from Primrose Hill, from Rowley Regis; from Quarry Bank, from Netherton, from Dudley. The hillock led them a dance, hiding

Mollie's path with hawthorn and with whin, with blackthorn and with bramble, but those with the persistence and patience to search were rewarded.

The reasons that Mollie's visitors had for making their journey were many and varied. A poor man came, leaning heavily on an ash staff. He had slashed his leg with a scythe while harvesting, it wouldn't heal and now he could barely work and his family were facing starvation. Mollie sat him down at her scrubbed wooden table, gave him a drink of herbs and honey and listened to his worries while she made him a poultice for his wound. A rich young woman came, wanting a charm to destroy the beauty of her rival in love, and thus secure the man's affections for herself. Mollie pushed her out of the door and threatened her with the same fate she had wished on the other woman if she ever returned.

The local doctor came.

Mollie stood at her door in the afternoon sun to receive him, and invited him to sit on the settle by the fire. She waited for him to speak.

'Mollie, I hear you have certain … abilities.'

Mollie said nothing.

The doctor cleared his throat and tried again.

'You have abilities, and you are a knowledgeable woman.'

Still Mollie waited.

'I am a man of science, but the thing is, I need help.'

Mollie nodded. 'That is the usual reason for people coming to see me. I have no quarrel with science. What is it that you need help with?'

'My son. He is 6 years old, and I fear his cough is killing him. He grows pale and thin, and he is so weak. I am a doctor, but I cannot help my own son.' The doctor sank his head into his hands.

'I will do what I can,' said Mollie, rising and crossing the room to a wall almost obscured by shelves, where she took her time scanning bottles and jars and cambric bags of dried herbs.

The sky was almost dark by the time the doctor left, his pockets full of herbs for teas, herbs for bathing and ointment for the child's chest, and his head full of the instructions Mollie had given him – and of something else she had said.

A few months later, Mollie died. There was much surprise; some thought she was immortal, but a man from Oldbury, calling to buy a cure for his cow, found her. She was definitely dead, as he told the minister at the local church, and the question was, what to do with the body. The churchgoers would not countenance her burial in their graveyard, and the minister was not inclined to contradict them. Eventually, it was decided to bury her in a murderers' graveyard at the crossroads at the bottom of the hillock.

There was no ceremony and no mourners at Mollie Mogg's funeral; in truth it was hardly a funeral at all, but only a burial. The church people lent their gravedigger, and that was all they would do for Mollie. That night, owls called from tree to tree across the lonely graveyard; foxes pawed gently at the newly turned earth; and a nightingale sang a sweet and bitter lament.

The doctor stayed at home. He was thinking, over and over, of what Mollie had said to him, and he didn't see how he could do it. She had helped his son over his illness, but how did he know that the boy wouldn't have got better anyway? Patients sometimes did, with no help; it was something every doctor knew. Casting his mind back to the evening that he had taken his leave of Mollie, he remembered an extraordinarily odd moment. As he turned to go, she had put her hand on his arm.

'There is one more thing,' she had said. 'I am destined to rise again in the form of a cat one week after my death. I want you to help me by opening my grave. I will wear a valuable ring; you may have it if you do this thing for me.'

With those words she turned and went inside her house, and he never saw her again. And now what was he to do? What could he do? He could not afford to be seen grave-robbing. He tried to put it out of his mind.

It seems that the doctor was not alone in knowing about Mollie's ring. The third night after her burial, three men sat in a tavern near the church that had shunned her, their heads together in a whispered discussion. One of them had heard a rumour about a valuable item in the coffin, but was afraid to dig it up on his own. A few strong drinks and their minds were made up. They went to each of their homes in turn to collect spades, then made their way to the crossroads.

A little later, the three of them, shoulder deep in the grave, heard the distinctive thud of a spade hitting wood instead of earth. They looked at each other, unsure about continuing.

'Come on, lads,' said one. 'We've come this far, no point in stopping now.'

So they scraped the earth away from the coffin lid and dug a little round the sides to make room to prise it off. Two of the men climbed out and the last forced the edge of his spade under the lid and twisted it. It started to come away; he moved his spade along and twisted again, and the lid was off. The two others leaned in to see what was there.

The coffin was empty. Mollie had needed no help after all. With a feverish, fumbling haste, the third man scrambled out of the grave and the three of them ran, fear and panic in their eyes.

Under a nearby tree was a black cat. She watched the men's desperate flight until they had gone from view, then she blinked slowly in the moonlight, stretched and walked away, the tip of her tail twitching.

ODE MAGIC

She lived in Cradley in Blue Ball Lane, and her name was to the point. Ode Magic. Yes, she was old, and yes, the people believed she had magic powers.

She made her living by selling spells, protective amulets, good luck charms, ointments and infusions with magical powers and cures for many ailments. Unlike Mollie Mogg of the last story, she was not at all reclusive, and she resembled nothing more than a particularly brash and uninhibited market trader.

Ode Magic used to leave her home in the mornings with a large covered basket over her arm. She walked the scant quarter of a mile to her accustomed pitch in Colley Lane, where there were likely to be good numbers of people passing. She had a favourite place to stand, a large flat rock that served as a stage and as a table to display her wares. Uncovering her basket, she spread out some of the cheaper and more eye-catching items on the rock, leaving the choicer and rarer commodities in the basket.

Then she climbed onto the stone, to wait for customers to come past. As people approached, she called out to them.

'Come along, my lovelies, come and see what I have for you today. Cures for your aches and pains. A little conjuring for what ails you. Wisdom where it's needed. Good luck charms – we all need a bit of that, don't we my dears?'

Ode Magic was well known to the people of Cradley, and she usually had one of three responses from her potential customers. Some would stop with a request for a medicine, or for something more occult. Some would wink as they passed. It was a code that meant there was a concern of a personal nature, and Ode Magic would receive a visit later at her home for a private consultation. Some would smile apologetically and say, 'Not today, thank you very much Magic. I'll have something another time,' and they would pass on their way.

What no one did, not if they had any sense, was to ignore Ode Magic, or to snub her. The woman had magical powers, after all, and she had been known to use them against anyone who offended her. There was the man hurrying to work who had no time, it seemed, even for a civil 'Good morning,' who that very day hit his thumb with a hammer and thus lost a week's pay while it healed. The young woman who flounced past, airing her view that Ode Magic was selling nothing but lies and rubbish, and who came down within the month with a nasty case of the pox. The chain-workshop owner, of whom we shall hear more shortly.

Cradley, like the neighbouring Cradley Heath, was for a long time a centre for the manufacture of chain – indeed it is often remarked that Cradley Heath is where the anchor chain for the *Titanic* was made. Men and women worked at this trade, hammering red-hot iron into links large and small. The hazards of handling the metal must be obvious, and the chain-makers were no less superstitious than anyone else in the Black Country, so Ode Magic had a steady stream of customers from amongst the workers, needing help with small injuries and wanting a supply of charms to ward off anything worse.

The owner of one of the workshops was a self-made man who had improved his station in life through his own hard work and wise investments. He considered himself above the irrational nonsense that his workers all seemed to believe in, and he thought of Ode Magic, at best, as an irritation. One day he was particularly preoccupied with a problem with running the shop. One of his suppliers wanted paying, and his biggest customer was yet to pay a large debt, and this was on his mind as he walked along Colley Lane.

There, as usual, was Ode Magic, hawking her nonsense for fools to buy, and she called out to the man: 'You look in need of a little cheering up my dear! Try my Gladness Pills. Only one a day, and the world is a different place!' She held out a small box.

'I don't need anything from the likes of you!' he shouted, inexplicably finding himself in a rage. He strode up to her and knocked the pill box out of her hand; the lid flew off and the pills were scattered across the road.

Ode Magic stared at him for a moment. 'Dearie me,' she said, quite self-assured. 'You will come to regret that.'

She said no more, and the man, knowing he should apologise but fearing it would look as though he was cowed by her veiled threat, turned on his heel and hurried away.

Nothing happened for a day or two. Then Ode Magic, each time one of the chain-makers passed her in the Lane, took on a sad and worried expression. The workers noticed her change in demeanour and began to talk amongst themselves as to what it might mean. They hesitated to ask her at first for fear of what she might say, but eventually a small deputation arrived at her stone to politely enquire if everything was all right.

'Oh, my dears, my dears, I do hope so. For a little while now I have been hearing vague portents from the Powers, nothing clear to begin with, but now —' she broke off and dabbed her eyes with a handkerchief, 'now, the signs are all there. There will

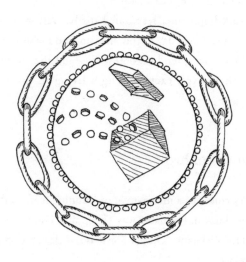

be a terrible accident in the chain shop, some time next week. Oh, my dears, I do hope you are going to be all right, but …' her voice trailed off.

The deputation urgently asked questions of the mystic: when would it happen? How could they avoid it? It became clear, from Ode Magic's answers, delivered between shuddering sobs, that the time could only be narrowed down to some time in the following week, and the only way to cheat fate was to stay away.

The workshop, of course, closed for a week, with a resulting loss of profit for the owner.

The next time he saw Ode Magic in Colley Lane, he stopped.

'I think I owe you for some pills,' he said.

'Yes, you do. Tuppence ha'penny,' was the not unkind response.

As Ode Magic took his money, she observed, 'The Powers. A law unto themselves. I'm so glad they only foresaw a week of trouble. It could have been a month.'

The workshop owner responded stiffly. 'Yes, well, that had occurred to me. Good day to you, madam, and I wish you well.'

Ode Magic accepted his good wishes and they both carried on with their lives, each making a living in the way they knew best.

The Dudley Devil

This story concerns a male witch, or 'cunning man' as they were sometimes known. His name was Theophilus Dunn, and how he acquired the nickname 'Dudley Devil' is not clear, but this story is based on fact.

He lived in Bumble Hole, Netherton, born into a family of mystics. As he grew, he was taught by his father to understand secret signs and portents, to learn spells and to employ his birthright, the skill of divination.

The young Theophilus took on the mantle of 'wise man' of the community, and to begin with, his fame was confined to the immediate area. But the industrialisation of the Midlands had an unexpected effect: the canals and roads that were built in the early nineteenth century to transport raw materials and finished goods were also effective in transporting people, and with them, ideas and stories. Thus, Theophilus's fame spread, and he found himself visited by clients from further and further afield: from London and even Scotland.

He had a reputation for being able to foretell the future, and to discover the location of lost or stolen items; he was also asked for simple advice. A local man was anxious to be rid of his wife, and, it has to be said, she of him. He consulted the Dudley Devil, asking what he should do.

In those days, divorce was not the 'done thing', but there was a practice that served a similar function, known as wife selling. It does seem that when this occurred, it was often by mutual consent, and also it was virtually the only way out of a marriage that was unsuitable for both parties, but nevertheless, there are no instances of which I am aware of husband selling, only wife selling. A man would tie a rope around his wife and lead her to the market; this was the conventional signal to indicate that the woman was for sale. When she was sold, this meant the end of the original marriage. Whether it meant a happier situation for the woman is uncertain.

Dunn, the Dudley Devil, gave the man some advice that he could have got for no charge in many other places, that is, to take her to the market and sell her. Perhaps the man felt the advice was more reliable for having cost money.

Theophilus Dunn's skill in finding lost or stolen items was based, some say, on skill in deduction rather than occult powers. There is a prediction he made, however, that remarkably came true.

It concerned William Perry, a boxer, also known by the name the Tipton Slasher. In 1850, at the age of 31, he became English Heavyweight Champion, having defeated Tom Paddock (the Redditch Needle Grinder). Perry was comfortably off, being not only a successful boxer but also the owner of The Fighting Cocks on Spon Lane, West Bromwich, but something must have made him wonder about the future because he went to consult Theophilus Dunn. Possibly it was just meant to be a bit of fun, but Dunn's words were ominous. Here they are as recorded by author Aristotle Tump:

Slasher, yo'll stop as yo' started
Yo'll get all yo' gid at one goo
Yo' an yer pub will be parted
Tom Little will mek it come true.

We can only wonder what William Perry made of this; there was no boxer named Tom Little, nor was there anyone who could lay claim to such a nickname. No doubt as the years passed, Perry put the prediction to the back of his mind.

In 1857, Perry was still the English champion. A fight was arranged with the young Tom Sayers, who was smaller than Perry with a fighting weight of just under eleven stones; indeed, the fight was billed as a 'David and Goliath' encounter. Perry was sure of winning, and of making a fortune on the fight. He mortgaged his pub and used the money to back himself.

William Perry, at the age of 38, was to prove to be past his best. Tom Sayers was younger, fitter, and, on the day, the better fighter. Perry lost the title and he lost his pub, as Dunn had predicted seven years before.

Perry took on the running of The Bricklayer's Arms in Walsall Road, Wolverhampton, so he had at least a home and an income.

Theophilus Dunn did not live to see his prediction fulfilled. He had died six years earlier.

10

SOME BLACK COUNTRY CHARACTERS

NANNY PIGGY

How Nanny Piggy got her name is a mystery, but from all accounts she deserved something far nicer. 'Nanny Piggy' stuck though, so 'Nanny Piggy' it was.

For years in Bilston market, Nanny Piggy ran a stall – part sideshow and part refreshment stall. Nanny made all of the snacks and sweets she sold, and every week her offerings would be the same, but no less popular for that.

She offered plates of that famous and well-loved Black Country dish, made with just two ingredients: bacon scraps and grey peas boiled together; balls of cooked rice known as rice knobs, fairly plain on their own but served with a treacle-and-water syrup poured over; nuts in a screw of paper; sticks of rock; and, to drink, sherbet.

She also had, at a ha'penny a shot, a spinning target game, which consisted of a horizontal rod fixed in a frame with simple wooden dolls threaded onto the rod. Nanny had painted the dolls to have bright clothes and smiling faces.

'Come up, my lovelies, have a go at my spinning game,' she would call out to the people passing by. 'Only a ha'penny a shot, and a prize every time!' The customer was given a wooden ball to throw, and they would try to set one of the dolls spinning. If they failed, Nanny gave them a small boiled sweet. Success would bring a choice of prizes: a little paper packet of sweets, or the chance to choose a folded slip of paper, which the winner would open to read their fortune. As Nanny Piggy was a kind old soul, and as Nanny Piggy was the author of said 'fortunes', the future would always hold something to the reader's benefit. 'Before the week is out, you will meet a stranger who will tell you something to your advantage' or 'The run of bad luck you have had will change. There is happiness in the future.'

Of course, Nanny knew all the people of the town – and especially the children, who used to flock around her stall, choosing what they would have for their penny or ha'penny this time. Nanny knew, too, that some were honest and some less so, and consequently it was not easy to play a trick on her. Occasionally, though, a cheeky ragamuffin might get away with it.

A lad approached Nanny's stall, and spent a long time perusing the goods on display. At last he seemed to make up his mind.

'How much are the rice balls, Nanny?' he enquired, with wide-eyed innocence.

'Same as always, my love, two for a penny.'

'Um. All right then, I'll have two rice balls.'

Nanny spooned the rice balls onto a saucer, and was just about to pour over the syrup when the lad held up his hand.

'No, I don't think I'll have the rice balls, I think I'll have some nuts.'

Nanny returned the rice balls to their dish and picked up a paper packet of nuts.

The lad almost took the packet, then he said, 'Do you know, Nanny, I don't fancy nuts today. I'll have a stick of rock, please.'

Nanny Piggy by this point was in no doubt that her leg was being pulled, but her face gave nothing away as she patiently placed the packet of nuts back on the tray, and offered the boy a stick of rock.

'Rock,' he said, casting his gaze heavenwards as if appealing for advice from above. 'Rock, do I want rock today?' He made up his mind with a triumphant smile: 'Nanny, I'm thirsty. I'll have some sherbet!'

Nanny Piggy gave him what is known as an old-fashioned look. 'You are a lot of trouble today, young man! Now are you quite sure?'

The lad assured her that he had finally made up his mind, and when Nanny handed him the glass of sherbet he drank it all down in one and started to walk away.

'Here!' said Nanny. 'You haven't paid me for the sherbet.'

The boy arranged his face into a hurt expression. 'Nanny! I swapped it for the rock.'

'But you never paid me for the rock!'

'No, of course I didn't, 'cos I swapped it for the nuts.'

'But you never paid me for the nuts!'

'Well, you gave me the nuts because I swapped them for the rice balls.'

'But you never paid me for the rice balls!'

With infinite patience the lad explained, 'No, I wouldn't have paid you for the rice balls, 'cos you took them back. They're in that dish. You don't expect me to pay for something you never give me?'

Nanny frowned. 'I know there's summat wrong. You got away with it this time, my lad, but don't you dare try that one again!'

And he didn't.

JACKY DINGDONG

His real name was John Westwood, but everyone knew him as Jacky Dingdong. He lived with his old wife Betty in a very modest little house next door to The Bell Inn. His nickname could have been a jocular reference to the pub, but it's more likely to have come from the cheeky street urchins of the town.

Jacky, in common with another character in this book, Edward Woolley, liked to affect old-fashioned eighteenth-century dress. When the other men of the town were wearing trousers that reached from waist to ankle, Jacky was still wearing knee-breeches. He wore a swallow-tailed coat, and the coloured silk stock that he wore around his neck might have accounted for the way he held his head, chin up, or perhaps that was a symptom of pride. His hair he wore in a plaited pigtail hanging down his back, years after it went out of fashion, and it did not pass unnoticed by idle boys in the street. It was a popular game, sadly, to run after Jacky, grab his pigtail and swing it, crying 'Ding dong!'

Jacky was a currier, a skilled worker. His job was to take tanned leather and dress it, finish it and colour it so it gained the suppleness and sheen that made it a saleable item. He could command higher wages than less skilled men, and it was a combination of that better pay, alongside a previous small inheritance and what might be thought of as meanness when choosing his own marital dwelling, that allowed him to invest his money in a number of properties in the town, which he rented out. He was a shrewd landlord and, as well as charging high rents, would ask his tenants before he agreed a tenancy what they had in the way of furniture and possessions. That way, if they failed to pay their rent and the bailiffs had to be sent in, he knew they would have something worth selling.

Jacky liked to be seen going to church on a Sunday, and he usually took his place in the gallery of St Leonard's for the start of the service. He did not, however, much enjoy the service itself, and he soon made his way quietly down the stairs once he had 'shown his face.' More on this later.

The stories told about Jacky all seem to revolve around his meanness with money. One Christmas, the local Methodist choir were carol singing in the town, raising funds for the church and for various good works. They came to Jacky's house and sang a carol outside his door. Jacky opened the door, and spoke in sweet tones.

'Your singing is lovely, just the thing to get a man in the right mood for Christmas. Will you come inside and sing another?'

As mentioned before, Jacky and Betty's house was not large, and there were twenty singers in the choir – but they were by now hungry and thirsty, and it was the usual thing to be offered refreshment when invited to sing in someone's home, so they all crammed into the front room. They sang another two or three of their best carols, and Jacky asked them to wait a moment while he went upstairs. They heard chinking sounds like the jingling of coins, then Jacky reappeared with a bag of money. He rummaged inside the bag and produced a penny, which he handed with some ceremony to the choir leader.

'There! That's for your collection. I won't detain you further, but make sure you call again next Christmas, won't you?' And he ushered them out.

Another little story shows Jacky in a very bad light. It might not be true.

Betty, like other women of her time, wore long dresses, and usually in the house she wore an apron over the top. One cold day, she and Jacky were keeping warm by the fire in the kitchen – the only fire in the house, due to Jacky's frugality, when Betty announced her intention to go shopping for a few essential supplies. She took a sovereign, there being nothing smaller in the

house, and put it in her pocket. She began to remove her apron but because of the cramped space she had to squeeze past Jacky, and her dress swept into the fire and caught light. As it flared up, she screamed to Jacky to help her. He sprang to his feet.

'Hold on, Betty! Just let me get that sovereign out of your pocket, then I'll put the fire out!'

As was typical of Black Country folk, Jacky was superstitious. One night he had a dream that frightened him, and when he woke up he resolved to pay a visit to one of his tenants, who had a reputation for clairvoyance and a special skill in interpreting dreams.

When Jacky went to see the man, he told him of his dream: he was at home, when there was a knocking at the door. When Jacky opened the door, there stood a fearsome creature – like a man but with flaming eyes, a snarling mouth and claws for hands.

'What does the dream mean?' Jacky asked.

The tenant took a slow breath and closed his eyes. He swayed slightly from side to side. At length he nodded sagely. 'Ah yes, I see it all. Your dream is a premonition. It's a warning of what is to come.'

'And what is to come?' gasped Jacky.

'The creature you saw is the devil. This time, you escaped. Next time, when he comes again, you may not be so lucky. He is watching you.'

'What does he want? Why is he watching me?'

The tenant took his time in answering. 'He sees the rents you charge. He has marked you to take away with him to the terrible depths.'

'But what can I do?'

The man tilted his head to the side, as if listening. 'The devil will return. He means to take you away – unless…'

The silence was terrible.

'What?' said Jacky in a strangled voice. 'Unless what?'

The man listened again. 'There is a glimmer of hope for you. If you lower the rents you charge to a reasonable level, then the devil will no longer have a hold over you. But be warned: you have very little time. He may come for you tonight.'

Jacky stuttered his thanks and immediately offered his tenant a reduction in rent. Then he hastened to all his other tenants with similar offers. All accepted. That night, Jacky slept well.

I mentioned that Jacky was a currier, and as a skilled worker he took on apprentices from time to time, perhaps two or three at once. He did not allow them any luxuries, but occasionally they contrived to help themselves.

One of the good Betty's many skills was in making country wines, from fruit and flowers she gathered herself in the fields and hedgerows surrounding the town. She made rose hip, dandelion and crab apple wines, to name but a few, but Jacky's favourite was elderberry. Betty kept her wines in small barrels in the cellar, and when Jacky fancied a drink, he would go down and turn the tap on a barrel to fill his glass.

He was usually vigilant at shutting up the house at night, including the window high in the cellar wall, but this one night he forgot. Perhaps he had been enjoying a little too much of Betty's wine. Thus it was that two apprentices wriggled their way into the cellar via the window, and there they found the best-tasting barrel and drained it. When Jacky went down the next day and tried to draw off a glass of elderberry wine, not a drop would appear. He shouted up the stairs to Betty.

'What's wrong, love?' she called back.

'The elderberry wine. It won't run!'

'Well turn the tap,' was Betty's reasonable rejoinder.

'I have turned the bloody tap! Nothing's coming out!' and Jacky continued in like vein, his language becoming more extravagant with his rising temper.

Betty tried to soothe him. 'Now Jacky, remember Job in the bible, how patient he was? Try and have a bit of patience, like old Job.'

Jacky exploded. 'Well he bloody well wouldn't have if he couldn't get a glass of wine when he wanted one!'

Jacky eventually came to a sad end. One Sunday, following his usual habit of leaving the church gallery a few minutes into the service, he stumbled at the top of the steps and fell down the whole flight. He died from his injuries. He may have been mean, but he wasn't a bad man, and it was a tragic end to his life.

The Man Who Could Whistle Like a Bird

Many years ago, in a little cottage in Willenhall Road, lived a former collier by the name of John. He had suffered an accident in the pit, which had ended his mining career and left him with an injured face, so that his mouth appeared twisted. In spite of this, though, he was expert at mimicking bird song; his face and mouth seemed not to move, but he could produce warbles, trills, calls and the most fluid bird-like melodies imaginable.

These days, we would not countenance the trapping of wild birds, but in John's time it was not unusual. In John's case, having lost his means of earning a living down the mine, dealing in birds kept body and soul together. He had a market stall where he sold songbirds: linnets and song thrushes he had caught, and canaries that he bred. The market rang with sweet song, either from the birds or from John himself.

One day Jon was sitting in a Wolverhampton inn. He was alone except for the caged linnet on the table beside him. From John's lips poured a mellifluous stream of notes, a perfect imitation of a linnet's song. The landlady, in the next room, heard the song and was entranced. She came through to listen more closely, but the music stopped as she entered.

'What a very pretty song!' she said. 'I would so love my customers to hear such a beautiful song. How much do you want for the bird? I don't mind how much I pay.' Now, as an opening to negotiations, that was perhaps not an ideal remark to have made.

John sighed sympathetically. 'It is a lovely song, isn't it? One of my best linnets. But this bird is already spoken for. I'm taking him to a man who is giving me a very good price for him.'

Knowing that someone else wanted the bird only made the landlady more keen. 'Whatever he's paying, I'll double it!' she said, not a little rashly.

John looked thoughtful. 'I'll tell you what I could do for you: I've got another bird that looks the same at home, and he's almost as good as this one. I could sell you this bird now, then go home and get the other bird for my customer. What do you think?'

The landlady was thrilled, and she hardly flinched when John named his price. She gave him the money, he handed her the cage, complete with bird, and he went on his way.

He never went back to the inn, and the bird never sang a

note. Well it wouldn't, would it? It was a hen. It's the cock birds that sing.

Lawyer Brown was a bird fancier, and he was very fond of songbirds. He called on John one day to tell him he was looking for a canary, a fine singer. In his little front room, John brought out a bird – a healthy well-coloured canary, singing lustily. John named a price.

Lawyer Brown examined the bird and said, 'It's a nice looking bird, and it sings well, but I know what you're like, John. You don't always show your best birds first. I don't mind telling you, I'd pay an extra half-sovereign for the right bird.'

John was reluctant. 'Hm. I suppose…you see, I do have another bird, and it is better than this one, but it's got a broken feather tip. It's caused no harm to the bird, and it'll sort itself out the next time the bird moults, but I don't like selling a bird that isn't perfect.'

The lawyer was keen. 'That doesn't matter John! You said it yourself – next time it moults, it'll be as good as new! Come on, let me see the bird.'

John left the room, cage in hand. He took the bird out, bent over the tip of a wing feather, returned the bird to the cage and took cage and bird into the front room where the lawyer was waiting.

Brown looked carefully at the bird. 'It is a little finer than the last, isn't it? I don't mind about the feather, John, I'll take it.'

Lawyer Brown paid John the original asking price, plus half a sovereign, and went away a happy man. The bird, this time, was a good singer!

11

STORIES OF THE UNEXPLAINED

Some years ago, I came across a story from Smethwick, set in the Rolfe Street baths. Sometimes when I tell it, I preface it with this Aynuk and Ayli story.

When Aynuk and Ayli were lads, Aynuk saw Ayli walking along the road with a rolled-up towel under his arm. Aynuk asked Ayli where he was going. Pausing to roll his eyes at his mate's stupidity, Ayli indicated the towel and said, 'I'm gooin' swimmin'.'

'Swimmin' in the cut (canal)?' enquired Aynuk.

'No! I'm gooin' to Rolfe Street baths. Why doe yo' come?'

'The baths?' said Aynuk. 'I cor (can't).'

'Why not? Bay (haven't) yo' got trunks?'

'Oh, ar, I got trunks. But I'm banned.'

'Banned?' said Ayli. 'Why am yo' banned?'

'Well, it's ockard (awkward), but…I piddled in the wairter!'

'Yo' piddled in the pool? That's not fair! Yo' shouldn't be banned. We all know we'm not s'posed to do it, but we all do!'

'Ar, but I was on the diving board at the time!'

Rolfe Street in Smethwick, the B4135, runs more or less parallel to the Birmingham Canal. Everywhere you look in the Midlands there is history just around the corner, and Rolfe Street is no different. The street itself looks ordinary, lined these days mostly with small factory units and garages, but just a few hundred yards' walk away along the canal is Galton Bridge, which in one structure links much of the area's industrial history. It is a Grade I listed building, designed by Thomas Telford, and when it was built in 1829 it was the highest single-span bridge in the world. It was named after Samuel Galton, the Birmingham arms manufacturer and member of the Lunar Society. The bridge was constructed from iron cast at the Horseley Iron Works in Tipton, near Dudley; the Horseley Works gained fame in 1821 for casting the world's first iron steamboat – many thought it couldn't possibly float. As it was assembled 130 miles away in Rotherhithe, it was possibly the world's first flatpack steamboat too.

While Galton Bridge was being constructed, in Rolfe Street and in many surrounding streets people were suffering. Decades before, hundreds had flocked from the countryside to the towns where they could find employment, but with overcrowded living conditions and a dire lack of proper sanitation, illness and disease were common. Not all the factory owners were blind to their workers' plight; the Chance factory was one that paid for improved living conditions for its workers, leading to an unsurprising improvement in their health. Most people's situations, though, were appalling and by 1832 there was an outbreak of cholera. Such was the concern of the authorities that public baths were built in Rolfe Street in 1888.

The baths were intended for the recreation and improved hygiene of the populace. There were two swimming pools, a municipal laundry, two showers and twenty-eight slipper baths. As almost all of the surrounding properties were built without bathrooms and many did not have indoor running water, the baths must have made a great difference to local people's lives, health and comfort.

THE SWIMMERS

In 1939, a young Smethwick couple were courting. Money was tight, and health and fitness was all the rage in the 1930s, so they used to meet at the Rolfe Street baths. The two of them swam side by side, matching stroke for stroke, turning as one at the end of the pool, striking out again to swim another length. Sometimes they swam in the mornings before work, just after the caretaker had unlocked the doors; sometimes they met in the evenings when the sun was setting, then, after their swim, they would walk to their homes under the stars.

At that time, the darkness was growing across Europe. Young men were joining the army and within a matter of weeks leaving England to fight in the war. The young man from Smethwick wanted to do his bit for his country, and when he talked to the young woman about it, as they walked hand in hand along Rolfe Street one evening, she was proud and afraid in equal measures.

It all happened so quickly. The young man joined the army, he was sent overseas, and he never returned. Only a few months after

their last evening in Rolfe Street, the young woman received the news.

She continued to swim at the baths. Perhaps it brought her comfort, perhaps she pretended to herself that he was still there, swimming beside her. Because she had trouble sleeping, she went to the pool early in the morning, the first to arrive, when the water was completely still. It was an odd sight, strange and eerie, the entire lack of movement; it looked almost as if the water was not there. The woman broke its surface with her first dive and struck out for the far side. As she swam, she had an uncanny sensation that someone was beside her. Turning her head, she saw splashing, as though there was another swimmer, but no one was there.

Every morning she would go to the pool to swim alone but strangely feel that she had company. Every morning now, the invisible swimmer was there beside her. One day as she was leaving the baths, the caretaker stopped her. He had something to tell her. He'd seen a young man in a soldier's uniform walking around the outside of the building, a young man who looked familiar. The young woman didn't know what to say. She nodded and thanked him, and went on her way, her head reeling.

Now, the young woman spent ever more time at the baths, swimming early in the morning, and wandering around the outside of the building, hoping to see someone who was never there. Then the day came when the caretaker found her, floating face down in the still water.

Perhaps it was an accident, but the woman was a strong swimmer. Perhaps she let herself drown so that she could join her young lover. We will never know, but the strange end to the tale is this: several times the first swimmers in the morning at the Rolfe Street baths saw not a perfectly still surface, but two tracks of disturbed water side by side along the length of the pool, just as if two swimmers were matching each other stroke for stroke.

The Rolfe Street baths were closed fifty years after the time of this story, in 1989. They were demolished, or rather, carefully taken apart, and resurrected in 1999 at the Black Country Living Museum, where the three-storey building is now the reception area and the exhibition hall. To end the story, there is one more ghost. Years ago, shops and businesses often had advertising signs painted on the brick wall at the end of the building. They were usually simply the name of the business, something like 'Black Country Iron and Steel Works' or 'Smith & Son Greengrocers'. Rolfe Street baths had its name painted high on the end wall, and it is still there at the building's current home. Over the years, the old painted signs faded, and some people make a hobby of collecting photographs of them before they fade away entirely. They are referred to as 'ghost signs'.

The Smethwick Recruit

Another story from Smethwick is set in the 1950s. Young men at that time went to serve in the armed forces under a scheme called National Service, also known as Peacetime Conscription, although the personnel concerned could find themselves under fire in areas of conflict across the world.

In the 1940s, a boy living in Windmill Lane was often to be seen playing with his friends in Victoria Park. With plenty of open space, it was a great place for games of football, kite flying and running around, and the trees were there, it seemed, to be climbed, and the bushes made a good secret den for the boys to share a bottle of pop and maybe the occasional biscuit snaffled from home. The boy used to walk to school across the park each morning, and on his way home, back across the park and along Ballot Street, he sometimes stopped, as did many of the other schoolchildren, at Mrs Peters' house. Now, whether this boy stopped or not depended on whether he had any pocket money left, because Mrs Peters ran a sweet shop. She had had her front door cut in half and hinged so that it flapped down to create a counter, and she sat in her wheelchair at her door, selling sweets to the local children.

Time passed, and the boy grew until he was old enough to be called up. He left his home for the first time and joined the army.

He did his two years' National Service, and as the time for his discharge came nearer, he found himself wondering if everything at home would look the same. At last he was released from duty, and he made the long journey home. Watching eagerly out of the window as his train drew into Smethwick Rolfe Street Station, he pulled his duffel bag down from the luggage rack and swung it onto his shoulder. Opening the door even before the train had stopped, he sprang out and almost ran across the platform. Out of the station, across the road and down along the High Street, where a walk of only a few minutes brought him in sight of Victoria Park. Hastening through the gates, he breathed in that old familiar scent of grass, flowers and trees. He saw a group of kids playing football, jumpers piled on the grass to make goal posts, and he smiled to think that would have been him only a few years before.

He reached the far side of the park and turned into Ballot Street, where he saw Mrs Peters, in her wheelchair as always, sitting at the door of her house ready to serve her young customers. He waved, and she waved back, but he was anxious to get home, so he didn't stop to chat.

Windmill Street, and home at last. His parents and sister were falling over themselves to welcome him in, and soon he was sitting on the sofa, in the front lounge that was kept for best, as if he was an honoured guest. His mother brought tea, and his sister, shy and proud in equal measures, carried in the cake she had made especially for him. The family had so many questions for him about where he had been, what he had done and the things he had seen. The young man found it hard to put it all into words, so great was the contrast between his army life and his home, at once so familiar and so strange. Eventually he came to his journey home.

'Do you know when I really knew I was home? When I saw Mrs Peters sitting in her doorway as always.'

His mother smiled. 'I remember so many Saturdays when you would pester me for just one more ha'penny so you could go and spend it at Mrs Peters'. I expect she was pleased to see you.'

The evening wore on and the young man, tired from his journey, was the first to go to bed. He again had that feeling, when he entered his old room, of it being so familiar and so strange, but he was very glad to be home, and it wasn't long before he sank into a restful sleep.

Downstairs, his mother looked at her husband. 'When do you think we should tell him that Mrs Peters died a year ago?'

A last story of the unexplained has a different setting in both time and place. I have remembered it as well as I can; I read it in a book that I can no longer find.

The Grammar School Boys

The school was in an old Midlands town and had been there so long that no one could remember a time before it was built. Indeed, it had an exceptionally settled air about it; the red brick was pleasantly worn and mellow, the stone lintels aged to a gentle old gold, the roof tiles fluted like a rippling sea captured in time, with even the gargoyles that guarded every corner seasoned almost to benignity. Between and around the buildings, paved stone paths seemed to sag in the centre, worn as they were by thousands of boys' feet over hundreds of years. The boys' dormitories, distanced from the main school by a covered walkway, nestled snugly by the perimeter wall, with clear polished leaded windows that looked out over wide green playing fields.

The schoolmasters (it was an all-male society apart from cook, matron and the school cat) wore mortar boards and academic gowns draped with narrow silk sashes, each different, striped with colours according to the master's old university and subject. The boys were sombrely arrayed, in deep grey trousers and long jackets, stiff white shirts with wing collars and black ties with a fine red stripe. The cat was tortoiseshell and white.

Sandy and Martin and Figgis and Tom were friends. They had started at the school together four years before; they shared a dormitory and they shared the joys and sorrows of school life. Snowball fights in winter; freezing on a muddy field in games lessons. The hard grind of long hours of lessons followed by prep; a free pass into town on a Saturday afternoon. The dreamy possibilities of a summer field trip; Latin lessons.

'Old Eely' was the Latin master, Mr Elysian to his face. Dreaded by all, his lessons were dull, repetitive, and to the four friends, meaningless. Latin was the last lesson on a Friday for the boys, and if their eyes drifted towards the window from time to time, and if, this particular Friday, knowing they had completed their prep for the week, their thoughts drifted to their Saturday afternoon outing, who could blame them? But all things come to an end, and eventually Old Eely released the boys from their torment. They packed up their books and escaped from the classroom with as much haste as was seemly. After tea in the refectory, they found a quiet spot in the common room to plan their trip to the town.

The next afternoon, Sandy, Martin, Figgis and Tom strolled towards the school gates and, as was their wont, paused for a moment on the threshold, savouring the taste of anticipated freedom. Then away! Swinging down to the town, with all the diversions and delights it offered.

They went, of course, for tea and buns, then, as they had agreed, to explore. The plan was to turn first left, first right, second left, second right and so on…and see where it got them.

The alley grew narrower until the boys had to walk in single file; all at once they found themselves in a dark little yard, overshadowed by buildings on each side, pale weeds growing between the paving slabs, and on the far side a cramped, crouching little shop. The only thing to do was to go in.

It smelt of dust, leather and old paper. It was hard to read the spines of the ancient books crowding the bowed shelves, so dim was the light inside. A pale man sat behind a wooden desk piled with sheets of curling parchment; a quill pen was in his hand. With so little space in the shop, it was impossible for the boys to feel unobserved. Sandy stretched out his hand and pulled a book from a shelf. Martin, Figgis and Tom huddled round as he opened it. The pictures! Even in the darkness, the colours glowed. There were dancers, wild and free, a castle that could not exist, weird landscapes, fierce untamed creatures and opposite each picture, intensely black writing that looked like Latin but that they could not understand. They had to have it.

'The price is two shillings and fourpence ha'penny,' said the man, rising and taking the volume from Sandy's hands. The boys shuffled to the dilute light near the grimy door, they dug their hands in their pockets and they pooled their remaining cash.

Exactly two shillings and fourpence ha'penny. The man had already wrapped the book in brown paper, string and sealing wax when they returned to him with the money.

Back at school, the boys agreed their classroom was the place where they were most likely to be undisturbed. In the fading late afternoon light and watched only by the school cat, they gathered around the book, laid open on the teacher's desk. They found one of the illustrations particularly compelling; it was of a single man-like creature, muscular, horned with scarlet skin.

All together, they read out the words on the opposite page, not understanding what they were saying. The cat arched her back, her fur standing on end. The air shimmered. The boys held their breath. There it was! It was there, in the classroom, the creature in the book. No blinding flash, no roar of thunder. One moment it was not there, then it was. The cat hissed, her ears laid flat. The creature turned its head, taking in the classroom, then its glare fell on the huddled boys.

'What do you want me to do?'

The boys managed nothing more coherent than a strangled squeak.

'What will you have me do? You summoned me. You must give me a task.' The creature's hands formed into fists, its body tensed.

Sandy found a tiny voice, 'We didn't mean – we haven't got a task.'

The others nodded their assent. The cat scrabbled desperately at the classroom door until she pulled it open a few inches, then she shot off up the corridor.

'If you have no task for me, I will make my own task. I will kill you.' It swung its heavy head from side to side, as if assessing which boy to destroy first. The boys scrambled to get behind the teacher's table. The creature picked it up and hurled it across the classroom. It crashed into the wall and splintered.

With a horrified fascination, the boys watched as the creature's eyes glowed red and it opened its mouth wider than seemed possible. It took a step towards them.

Just at that moment the door flung open and the cat came tearing in, followed by Old Eely. Black gown flying, eyes wild, he flung a pointing finger at the creature and spat a stream of words at it. Latin, the boys dimly recognised through their terror. The thing roared, it writhed, it screamed – and was gone.

Sandy, Martin, Figgis and Tom were of course refused leave to go into town for the rest of the term. The teacher's desk was mended. The boys never did get to like Latin lessons. But at least now they could see the point of it. The question they could never answer, though, was who, exactly, was Old Eely?

12

HIGHWAYMEN AND HIGHWAYWOMEN

And still of a winter's night, they say, when the wind is in the trees,
When the moon is a ghostly galleon, tossed upon cloudy seas,
When the road is a ribbon of moonlight over the purple moor,
A highwayman comes riding –
Riding – riding –
A highwayman comes riding, up to the old inn-door.
(from 'The Highwayman' by Alfred Noyes)

Highwaymen are figures of romance in the popular imagination; the very word conjures up a dashing image of a man (or woman) on horseback. Alfred Noyes describes the highwayman of the poem as dressed in a claret velvet coat, perfectly fitted doe-skin breeches, boots up to his thighs, lace at his neck and a French cocked hat on his head. He carries pistols and a rapier, the tools of his trade. The highwayman: a romantic hero, a ruthless armed criminal, or both?

The following stories suggest something of the fantasy and something of the reality of the lives of these Gentlemen of the Road.

ROWLEY JACK AND REBECCA FOX

The road from Whiteheath Gate to Dudley ran north-east through some wild and lonely hills and heathland. Abraham Fox was owner and smith at the Whiteheath forge, which also served as a hostelry for travellers on the road to Dudley and beyond. It was known to be a haunt of footpads and highwaymen, and anyone journeying as night was falling, whether riding alone, with a companion or on a stagecoach, was glad to see the welcoming lights of Fox's forge as well as the welcoming smile of his comely daughter Rebecca.

Abraham Fox offered the travellers stabling for their horses, ale to drink, meat to eat and a bed for the night. Rebecca Fox served the drinks, brought the platters of food and engaged their guests in lively conversation. She talked of the guests who had stayed at the forge before; the travellers talked of their own travels. As Rebecca brought more ale, she playfully tried to guess where the travellers might be going and why; she was always wildly wrong and the men (it was almost always men) corrected the silly young woman. With yet more ale, Rebecca teasingly talked, in a confidential whisper, of the wealth and the valuables carried by the fine men who had stayed with her father before and how she, a simple country girl, was dazzled by what they had showed her; the men were soon taking out the contents of their pockets and purses, wanting to be the one who most impressed the lovely and charming, if rather witless, serving girl.

When all had retired to bed, Rebecca changed into greatcoat and breeches and slipped quietly out to the stables. Saddling one of her father's horses, she mounted and rode away.

Rowley Jack was notorious in the Rowley and Dudley area as a ruthless but elusive highwayman. The roads were hilly, and lone riders and coaches alike frequently had to slow their pace as their way became steeper. It was at these points that Rowley Jack lay in wait, ready to ride out and challenge the travellers with pistol and sword. Mostly they escaped unharmed, but with their pockets and saddlebags considerably lighter; reaching Dudley, Rowley Jack's prey complained to the authorities. Constables were sent to track him down; they made many attempts to follow his horse's hoofprints, but Jack always proved hard to find. There was something odd about the horse's tracks, the men reported. They never seemed to lead the way the constables expected, and always petered out on a stretch of flinty ground. Rowley Jack remained at liberty.

Jack took his horse to be shod by one blacksmith, and one blacksmith only. Abraham Fox made unique shoes for his customer and confederate; Rowley Jack's horse had double shoes – normal shoes, nailed to the horse's hooves, and a second set, welded underneath the first set and facing the other way. To anyone seeing the hoofprints, the horse was walking backwards.

The highwayman lived in an isolated cottage; he had plans for a grander life, once he had accrued enough wealth. With episodes of action and excitement, his life on the whole was quiet, and it was on one of his quiet nights at home that he heard the sound of a horse outside, followed by a knocking at the door. He smiled when he heard the rhythm of the knocks; he rose and strode to the door, welcoming Rebecca inside and taking her in his arms. She kissed him and led him to the settle, where they sat while she reeled off descriptions of the men staying at the forge and of what they were carrying and where it would be hidden.

'My darling, my dear, clever girl,' he said. 'Soon we will be leaving this life together.'

Neither of them was aware of the truth of his words.

Before dawn, Rebecca slipped out of Jack's bed and hurried back to her father's house before any of the guests knew she had gone.

Eventually, the Dudley constables realised what it was that was strange about the horse's tracks. The men Jack had challenged on the road gave reports of the direction he had taken as he made off with their valuables; the reports never tallied with the evidence of the visible tracks. It must be the horse's shoes, and that meant a complicit blacksmith.

The constables found a hiding place where they could watch Abraham Fox's forge. For days nothing happened. The men worked in shifts, approaching and leaving the hide by a circuitous route to avoid attracting attention. At last, one night, a man on horseback and matching Rowley Jack's description arrived at the forge and went into the stables. As the constables watched, a figure dressed in male attire, but apparently a young woman, appeared from the house and followed the man into the stables. The constables, afraid to go inside and confront Jack at close quarters, drew their firearms and shouted for the pair to come out and show themselves.

A horse carrying two riders sprang from the stables and in moments was galloping away. In the saddle the constables saw Rowley Jack, and behind him, her arms around his waist and pressing into his back, was a young woman. The men held their fire for fear of wounding the woman. They scrambled back to their hiding place and mounted their horses, but Jack and Rebecca had too much of a start on them, and after a fruitless pursuit they fell back on lighting lanterns and searching for tracks.

Their suspicions about the horse's shoes were confirmed, but again the backwards-facing tracks petered out on harder ground, and Rowley Jack and his lover made their escape. Abraham Fox was arrested as an accomplice, but he had to be released because of lack of evidence.

Rebecca and Rowley Jack had disappeared, and it was assumed that they had made their way to a distant part of the country and were living on the spoils of their crimes. Nothing more was heard of them until twelve years after their disappearance.

A local historical society was exploring a ruined fourteenth-century building, Tividale Hall, when they found a passage leading to cellars underground. The passage had been blocked but the society members laboured to remove the fallen masonry – and were shocked at what they found. The skeleton of a horse lay stretched out on the floor, still with its saddle and bridle, and beyond that, huddled against a pillar, were two human skeletons, both wearing the remnants of male dress. One, the larger, was a man, and he had his arm around the smaller skeleton, a woman, whose head nestled against his chest.

The authorities in Dudley were informed, and an examination of the horse's shoes confirmed the obvious conclusion. Rowley Jack and Rebecca Fox had been found.

Tividale Hall was finally demolished in 1927. The site where it stood is in a central location in Tividale, opposite the Co-op, but nothing now remains of either the hall or the fateful underground passages.

Jonathan Wild

Even today, Boningale, just west of Wolverhampton, is tiny: a pub, a few houses and farmland. What must it have been like in Jonathan Wild's day? Bound apprentice in Birmingham, it did not take him long to become accustomed to town life; to a country boy, the pace and excitement of his new home was intoxicating.

He met a young servant girl and, carried along by his euphoria, he asked her to marry him. Soon they had set up home together in a little rented garret, and a few months later Mrs Wild gave birth to a baby boy.

There is a saying about marrying in haste, and Jonathan Wild proved it to be true. He soon began to spend more and more time in the tavern, and less and less time with his wife and baby.

While out drinking one night, Jonathan got into conversation with two men who were passing through Birmingham on their way back to London. Jonathan talked of how exciting he found town life, compared with his earlier years living in a tiny hamlet. The two men looked at each other.

'If you like Birmingham, you'll love London,' said one.

The second man agreed. 'It's a glorious place, lad. The buildings are grand enough to take your breath away, there's crowds of people – lots of them are pretty girls – and,' he leaned in close, 'there's plenty of money to be made.'

The two warmed to their topic, describing the joys and delights of the theatres, the parks, the astonishing new cathedral that dwarfed Birmingham's St Martin's ('Not that we go inside, you understand').

Jonathan's mind was made up. 'When you go on your way tomorrow,' he said, 'can I come with you?'

The men agreed, and the meeting place was arranged.

He returned to his lodgings and slipped into bed beside his wife to catch a few hours' sleep before his new adventure began. In the stillness before dawn, he rose again and by the light of a single candle he looked for the last time on the faces of his family: his wife, fair curls escaping from her white cotton cap, her chest gently rising and falling, rising and falling under the buttons and lace of her nightgown; the baby, safe in his cradle, dark lashes edging his closed eyes, his lips parted as he murmured in his sleep. The baby's father turned away and opened a chest at the foot of the bed. He took out his few items of clothing and a small bag that held the money he and his wife were saving together. He tied it up in a bundle with his clothes and then he was out of the door, down the stairs and out into the street.

A little later, he met his new friends and all three set their faces to the south.

The journey took several days, and it was not too long before Jonathan realised he was being taken for a fool. They stopped for refreshment several times that first day, and each time the two men waited for Jonathan to pay; 'We'll pay next time, so it'll be fair.' So early the next morning Jonathan set off before his companions were awake, with a new feeling of freedom and with the coin he had taken from the men's pockets weighing down his own.

But they had told him the truth about London. It was everything they had said and more, the sights, the sounds, the smells and the river! The river was a revelation, and watching the ships and boats so full of goods and passengers gave him an idea.

First, though, he must see about attiring himself. He wandered around the city until he came to a tailor's shop and there he bought a velvet coat in an eye-catching bright blue and a fine silk shirt. At a bootmaker's he chose a pair in a glossy black made of fine Spanish leather, then on to a horse dealer's where he bought a white mare.

Securing lodgings in a fine house with views of the park, he settled into London life. A fine-looking young man, expensively dressed, it was easy to get credit, and even easier to run up bills he couldn't pay. Rent, stabling for his horse, food, drink and gambling – all conspired to drag him deeper into debt and inevitably he was arrested and sentenced to a debtors' prison, the Fleet.

It was in prison that his luck took a turn for the better or the worse, according to how you look at it. He met a woman, Sal, a little older than himself, who proposed to him the plan of making a life together as highway robbers. Jonathan considered the proposal and countered it with a better one.

'What do you say you and I set up in business dealing the goods that are acquired by highway robbers? They want rid of them, we can sell them on. A few quiet words in the right ears and we shall be making money from others' risk.'

They sealed their deal with a kiss, bribed a guard with promises, and they were free. They set up shop at an inn by the river, and with Sal's underworld connections and her skill at writing up careful accounts, and Jonathan's silver tongue, they soon had a thriving business. They had money to spend and money to save, and life was good except that for Jonathan Wild, London was starting to feel rather small. One night as they danced together to the tune of a fiddler under the light of a dying moon, Jonathan told Sal of his grand plan. They would buy a ship and a crew and take their gold and diamonds on a trip to see the wonders of the world. Sal laughingly agreed.

The ship was soon bought and prepared for a voyage, while Sal and Jonathan closed their business, paying what was owed and selling the last few goods. On the morning of their departure Sal left early, saying she was going down to the ship to make their quarters ready. Jonathan was about to leave when the door flew open and three constables rushed in, pinning him down before he had a chance to think.

The case was heard at the Old Bailey, and it was watertight. The authorities had somehow got hold of Jonathan's account books, showing his vastly profitable dealings in stolen goods. The account books showed no accomplice, but explicitly named only Wild. He was sentenced to be hanged at Tyburn. Sal, of course, did not see the hanging. She was on her way to Spain on the deck of her own fine ship with the sea swell beneath her and the soft wind in the sails. She had enough riches to last her a lifetime. Enough riches for one.

The Restless Servant

A rich man had a young housekeeper who was capable and unflappable in spite of her youth. The man admired the young woman: her intelligence, her self-possession, her good humour. Truth be told, the man was not much older than his housekeeper, as his parents had died and he had inherited their estate at a young age. He found himself, more and more, thinking out loud about his concerns when the young woman was in the room, and she found herself, more and more, giving thought to what he had said. Later, perhaps when tidying his study or bringing him his meal, she might say, as if to herself, 'I remember a summer like this a few years ago. They got the crops in early, and avoided a drenching,' or 'They do say the land on the edge of the town could be bought for a good price. People are needing houses,' and then she would go about her business.

The man began to think how wonderful it would be to have a wife who was in every way his equal. A woman of intelligence, self-possessed and with good humour, who could understand his problems and help him to solve them. Not his housekeeper, of course. A wife would have to be his social equal as well.

One morning, the young man was surprised to see his housekeeper with her coat on and a travelling bag in hand.

'I'm off,' she said.

'Off?'

'Off. To seek my fortune. I rather fancy the life of a footpad.'

'Footpad?'

'Indeed. A highwaywoman. I'll be a footpad until I have enough money to buy a horse.'

The young man opened his mouth to say something, he knew not what, but the woman turned and was gone.

She went out to the highway and walked. She whistled, she sang, she swung her arms as she strode to meet her destiny. After an hour or more a man on horseback overtook her. He wore a three-cornered hat and a flowing black cloak and his horse was very fine. He greeted her with a devilish smile.

'And where are you going on this fine day, a maid all alone?'

She looked up, squinting into the sun. 'I thought, kind sir, that a life as a footpad would suit me better than a life as a servant. I'm off to seek my new life.'

The man's devilish smile gave way to a guffawing laugh. 'Seeking a life as a footpad, is it? Well you've met the right man. I,' he raised his hat in mock courtesy, 'am Turnpike Tom, the most feared highwayman in these parts.'

The young woman brightened. 'Aha! Then you can advise me, sir, since it seems that we are brother and sister outlaws. How... how exactly do I go about robbing rich folk on the road?'

He laughed again and looked at her thoughtfully. 'Since, as you put it, we are brother and sister outlaws, I will give you some advice. If a man you wish to rob is walking, knock him down. If he is riding, knock him off his horse. If he ventures to speak, kick him and say, "Silence, cur! Hand me your money and your valuables or it will be the worse for you!" and threaten him with your pistol. Then you take what you can and ride off.' He paused for a moment.

'Only, it seems that you have neither a pistol nor,' he made a show of looking around, 'a horse. The best thing you can do is throw your lot in with me. I could make great plans for the two of us.' He gestured to a wayside inn further along the highway. 'Come and have a drink with me, and we can talk.'

She dropped a curtsey. 'Thank you kindly sir, but I do not enter such establishments. I must continue on my way, and I wish you good day.'

The highwayman laughed again, and as he urged his horse on, he said, 'As you wish. A few more miles of walking might change your mind. I will catch up with you later.'

As the woman carried on her way, she watched Turnpike Tom ride to the inn, dismount and go inside. Her journey carried her on past the place where Tom sat drinking and further on until the road passed through a patch of woodland. She searched until she found a fallen dead branch, and hitching up her skirt and petticoat, she climbed a roadside tree, hauling the branch up with her. She waited, making herself as comfortable as she could on a horizontal bough.

Hidden amongst the green leaves, the young woman watched as a number of travellers passed, some on foot, some mounted. None of them looked rich. She let them go, and they were forever unaware that they had been observed.

At last, a man on a fine horse rode towards her. He had a three-cornered hat and a flowing black cloak. He was singing a smutty song. The young woman carefully renewed her grip on the dead branch, and, waiting until the last moment, let it swing down under its own weight. The end caught the rider a cracking blow on the side of the head and knocked him off his horse, which cantered away into the woods.

Tom blinked and looked blearily up at her. 'You! How dare —' but he got no further.

'Silence, cur!' She aimed a swinging kick which found its mark, and as he grunted and folded up, she snatched the pistol from his belt. She cocked it.

'Your money or your life!' she cried.

His eyes watering, he gasped, 'In my saddlebags.'

The woman relieved him of a couple of items, then she whisked away, picking up her bag from behind the tree and following the path the horse had taken.

The young man left at home was feeling bereft. The sudden departure of his housekeeper had come as a shock, and he found himself that day unable to settle to anything. He kept drifting towards the window and looking out, just in case. Then he would go to the door and open it. Just in case. Several times he wandered out onto the road, shading his eyes to look along it. Just in case. He had sat down at his desk to try and concentrate on some correspondence, when he heard a clattering of hoofs in the yard. Rushing outside, he was brought up short by the sight that greeted him.

A figure with a three-cornered hat and a flowing black cloak with a pistol in her belt was mounted on a fine horse.

'I have,' she said, as she swung her leg over the horse's neck and slid to the ground, 'a fine horse, a pistol, something in excess of a hundred gold coins and sundry other valuables, and the man who gave them to me is not in a position to ask for them back. I am therefore a woman of property, and it is my firm belief that you and I should marry.'

The young man stared blankly for a moment.

'All right then,' he said.

Did the young woman henceforth give up her life of crime? That is another story!

13

WISE FOOLS

All countries and regions seem to have their Wise Fool or Noodlehead stories, and often there is a particular town where the Noodleheads are reputed to reside. Poland has Chelm, Nottinghamshire has Gotham, the West Midlands has Darlaston. In all cases, of course, the reputation is unfair; the people of Chelm, Gotham and Darlaston are as sensible as anyone else, but that's how folklore works. So, with profound apologies to the people of Darlaston, here are stories of fools, some wise, some otherwise.

MET HIS MATCH

An old Darlaston lawyer used to meet with many of the town's workers in the pub of an evening, and he liked to share a joke with his companions.

One evening, he found himself seated next to a nail-maker, and they got into conversation. The nail-maker, after a few drinks, and perhaps unwisely, began to hold forth on the tricks and dodges that nail-makers used to get up to in an effort to squeeze a little

more money out of their employer and add a little to their meagre
wages. Ways of making a bag of nails weigh more, how to get more
nails out of a length of wire, and so on.

The lawyer, not unsympathetically, shook his head.

'Ah, you'll never get to heaven, Tom,' he said.

The nail-maker returned with, 'Then let me tell thee a story.'

The lawyer took a sup of his ale and prepared himself to
be entertained.

'There was a nail-maker, I knew 'im well, and 'e died. So 'e
meks 'is way up to 'eaven, and there's St Peter on the gate. St Peter
looks 'im up an' down an' says, "No, lad, this is not the place
for thee, thou'll 'ave to goo downstairs, to th'other place." The
nail-maker, 'e argues and protests, but St Peter, 'e's 'avin' none
of it. Just then, there's a whole load o' people rushin' in through
the gates, thee knows, nurses an' colliers an' factory owners an'
the like, an' the nail-maker, 'e pushes into the middle of 'em,
an' gets carried through. Well! What was St Peter to do then? So
when 'e's finished ticking off all the others who are on 'is list, 'e
turns to the nail-maker again. "Well, you've got yourself in, but
who's goin' to plead your case to let you stay?" The nail-maker
says, "Can I stay until I find a lawyer, I know nuthin' about the
law meself." So St Peter agrees, the nail-maker can find himself a
lawyer to plead his case. An' dost thou know, that wuz ten year
ago, an' 'e's still lookin'!'

The lawyer, who of course knew how that story would end as
soon as it started, as did we all, was not so much of a noodle that he
didn't laugh with a good grace.

THE DARLASTON FAIR

A long time ago, the annual fair was one of the highlights of the year. Part livestock market, part pleasure fair, it attracted great numbers of people from the area for three days at the end of April.

A woman ventured out to join the crowds on the final day. With stallholders shouting for attention on either side of her, she didn't know where to go or where to look next, when one particular stall caught her eye. It was a coconut shy, but look! There were such darling little prizes! Dolls, pottery figures, pin boxes, combs, ribbons ... she would have liked to win any of them.

She paid her penny and took the three wooden balls the man handed her. The first two balls went wide, with not a hope of even making contact with a coconut, let alone knocking one down. The third one would have gone the same way, but a passer-by knocked the woman's elbow and the ball shot out of her hand before she meant to let go of it. It flew straight, fast and true, it smacked into the coconut with a loud crack, and the coconut flew into the air, thudding down onto the grass.

The woman was quite overcome; she had never won anything before, and she had to take a moment or two to gather herself. The man gestured to the array of prizes, and the woman, still breathless, began the difficult task of choosing between such desirable items. After a moment, something she had not noticed before caught her eye: it looked like a little picture, about the size of the palm of her hand, with an ornate frame and a handle. That is what she chose, and she bore it home, thrilled and delighted.

Once home, she took it out and looked at it; she was amazed to see that it was a picture of her mother. She looked again.

'No! It's me grandmother!' she exclaimed. She was very perplexed to see a family portrait on a picture won at a fair; she couldn't understand how it could have happened and she put the picture away in the bedroom drawer while she pondered some more.

Later on, her husband came in while the woman was busy preparing the evening meal, and he rummaged in the drawer, searching for a piece of string to use as a shoelace. He found the picture and, taking it out, he held it up to look at it. At first he was puzzled, then he became angry. He went storming into the kitchen.

'It's bad enough,' he said, 'that yo've got yourself a fancy man. It's bad enough that yo' keep a picture of 'im in our bedroom drawer. But it's the final insult that yo' choose a man so damned ugly!'

The rift between them was finally healed when a kind friend explained what a mirror was.

The Clicking Toad

A man was travelling through the Midlands by stagecoach, which stopped for a while in Darlaston. It was a pleasant late afternoon in August, and the man thought he would take advantage of the stopping place at the edge of the town bordering a stretch of open countryside. He lived in the city of Birmingham, and it gave him great pleasure to feel the grass under his feet, to smell the scent of wild flowers and to listen to the birds twittering and singing in the bushes and trees.

It had been a warm day, and much of the warmth still lingered, so as he walked he removed first his jacket and then his waistcoat. Strolling along, searching for bilberries or blackberries to quench his thirst, he didn't notice his large round pocket watch slip from his waistcoat and land gently in the soft grass. It was a fine watch, with a pearl face and slender hands and a good tick, but now it was lost in the grass.

The man sauntered back to the coach just as the other passengers were boarding, and he had travelled several miles before he missed his watch.

Meanwhile, two men were walking the same path he had trod, on their way home from harvesting in the fields. It was that lovely

time on a late summer's evening, when the light is beginning to fade from the sky and a beautiful stillness is settling over the countryside. Sensing the peacefulness of the moment, the men walked in a companionable silence, when their attention was caught by a strange clicking noise. Searching around for the source of the disturbing sound, they saw what they thought was a round white eye, staring at them, unblinking and awful.

'What is it?' whispered one man to the other.

'I doh know! But I doh like it. It's got an evil look in its eye.'

'And listen to the terrible noise it's mekkin',' went on the first man. 'Sounds like it's workin' itself up. What's it gonna do?'

'I doh know, but it's a nasty little thing, that's for sure. We better get help.'

The men started walking away, but soon broke into a run – well, it might be after them.

Back home, they told everyone they met about the clicking thing with the big eye. A group of concerned townsfolk installed themselves in the bar of the Spread Eagle for a conference. A few brave souls ventured out to look at it, carrying lanterns now that it was almost dark. They found the evil one, just as it had been described: it fixed them with a cold stare and clicked menacingly. Thoroughly unnerved by their experience, they ran back to the Eagle. After further debate, someone had an idea. They should all go to the wise man and ask his advice.

The wise man lived on the outskirts of the town in a one-roomed cottage. The people all tried to cram in, but there wasn't the room, so the wise man came to the door and listened carefully to them as they stood in the road.

'I must see the creature for myself,' he said. He had grown wise by living a long time; in deference to his advanced age a wheelbarrow was brought to transport him to the field.

The procession was a solemn and silent one, led by the wise man reclining in his chariot, his legs dangling on either side of the wheel. As they neared the creature, they could all clearly hear the ominous clicking. The wise man asked to be wheeled around the evil one so that he could get a good look.

He asked to go round twice more, then addressed the crowd.

'It is a clicking toad! A clicking toad! Run, run for your lives! It comes to bring destruction upon you! Flee!'

Flee they did, the man with the wheelbarrow running as best he could and courageously suppressing the desire to leave the wise man in the barrow and chase after the rest of the crowd. Once home, everyone bolted their doors and shuttered their windows and awaited their doom.

Early the next morning, a man alighted from the mail coach. He followed the path he had taken the day before and, with a little searching, found his pocket watch, wet with dew but still gamely ticking. He polished it with his handkerchief, put it in his pocket and went on his way, whistling.

The Wheelbarrow

An inspector, visiting a building site in Darlaston, saw a man wheeling a wheelbarrow upside down. He watched the man for some time as he crossed from one side of the site to the other, sauntering along, all the time with his barrow upside down.

Eventually, the inspector went over to him and asked him what he thought he was doing.

'Ah, well that's the point,' said the man.

'What point? What do you mean?' asked the inspector

'I'm not really doin' anythin'. If the barrow wuz the right way up, they'd have me carryin' things in it!'

The Bricklayer

A man was hired to build a brick shed on a farm just outside Darlaston. He looked up from his work and saw a farm labourer crossing the yard. Having heard about the Darlastonians and their silliness, he thought he'd have a bit of fun at the man's expense.

'Hey,' called the bricklayer to the labourer. 'Do yo' 'ave chickens on this farm?'

The labourer stopped and regarded the man gravely. 'We do,' he said.

'Well,' said the bricklayer, suppressing a snigger, 'how many eggs do the cockerels lay?'

The labourer strolled over to the bricklayer and ran his eyes over the wall he was building. 'Not many. But our cockerels are better at layin' eggs than yo' are at layin' bricks.'

Another Wheelbarrow

Sent to collect a new wheelbarrow from Wednesbury station, a Darlaston labourer went via his home to collect his own

wheelbarrow. At the station, he carefully placed the new barrow on top of his old one and set off, taking care not to unbalance his precarious load. When he finally got to the building site, the foreman watched him incredulously, then asked him what he was doing.

The man was sullen.

'Why should I wheel a new barrow all the way from the station? Yo' can't mek me!'

Too Short

The Bishop from Lichfield was making a tour of the churches in the diocese, and this day he was visiting Darlaston. He decided to spend some time walking around the town and meeting its people and he was strolling down a residential street in the more well-off side of town when he saw a small boy standing at one of the front doors. The boy was intermittently jumping up and down, making, it seemed, great efforts to reach something. As the Bishop drew closer, he could see that the boy was attempting to reach the doorbell. The Bishop noticed two ladies approaching on the other side of the road, and wanting to impress them with his kindness and charity, he went up to the boy and said, 'Can I assist you, my boy?'

The boy had clearly been taught good manners, for he replied meekly, 'Yes, please, sir, I'm a-trying to reach the bell.'

With a glance towards the ladies, who were now quite close and well within earshot, the Bishop said, 'Certainly, my child, here you are,' and he gave the bell a good long press.

'Thanks mister!' said the boy. 'Now run like 'ell!'

The Way to Heaven

Silas the gun-lock maker and John the nail-maker were enjoying a drink in the Spread Eagle. They talked of this and that, and as the evening drew on Silas became thoughtful.

'We'm good men, ay we, John?'

'Ar, I s'pose we am,' said John.

'I mean, we've both got jobs, an' we work 'ard.'

John agreed.

'An' we doh do nuthin we shouldn't.'

John gave this last statement some thought. 'Well not much, anyway,' was his opinion, 'not often. Not as often as some.'

'So, what I'm thinkin' is,' Silas paused to sup from his tankard, 'we'll be gooin' to 'eaven.'

'When we die, yo' mean?' said John, for clarity.

'When we die, yes, but I was wonderin', why not goo up there an' check. You know, jus' 'ave a word wi' 'em, see 'ow it's gooin'.'

'Wot yo' mean, Silas? Yo' can't goo 'afore yo'm jed (dead)!'

'Ah,' Silas nodded sagely, 'that's wot I bin thinkin'. My sister's bloke's a builder, an' I thought, 'e'll lend us 'is ladders. We con tie two or three together, an' get up to 'eaven that way. Mebbe one of us goes up, an' one of us stands at the bottom wi' 'is foot on the ladder, 'oldin' it safe, like.'

John nodded. 'Ar, it 'ud be a shame to fall off an' die on the way. Then where wud yo' be?'

'That is exactly my thinkin'. So 'ow about it? Will yo' 'elp me?'

John agreed that he would help Silas, and the plan was put into effect. Silas borrowed the ladders from his brother-in-law, John borrowed some string from work and the ladders were tied together. The two men were surprised at how unwieldy three ladders tied together actually were, but after a few false starts and considerable retying and repositioning of the string, they managed to swing the ladders upright and with John taking a firm steadying grasp, Silas started his ascent.

John tipped back his head to watch Silas's progress. His tread was firm and he rose and rose from rung to rung until John lost sight of him among white fluffy clouds. He waited patiently while an hour passed, and at last he felt a vibration in the ladder and sure enough, Silas was descending.

John could hardly wait for his friend to reach the ground.

'Well?' he said. 'What 'appened?'

Silas leaned on the ladder to catch his breath for a few moments.

'Yo' wouldn't believe it. I got up there, an' there were the gates o' 'eaven, with Saint Peter an' all, only it looked jus' like the bar in the Eagle. No kiddin'. There wuz Peter, standin' be'ind the bar, jus' like the ol' landlord duz, theer wuz even the chalkboard where they keeps tally on the wall be'ind the bar.'

John was amazed. 'Blimey!' he said. 'An wot did Peter say?'

''E asked me what I wuz doin' theer, an' me not jed, an' I sez I woz jus' mekkin' enquiries, like, to see 'ow I'd be fixed when me time comes. So 'e takes a piece o' chalk, an' 'e sez, "Well let's see, then," an' 'e starts writing all me wrongdoin's on the board.'

'Cor!' said John. 'An' am yo' all right then? Did Peter say they'll let yo' in?'

'I dunno yet. I jus' come down fer more chalk!'

THE RED-HOT SHILLING

A woman was walking from Moxley to Pleck one fine day, and as she approached Darlaston, she chose a route which took her along a lane bordering farmland. The lane was winding and edged either side with tall dense hedges, so she was surprised on rounding a bend to see a group of people, all clustered in a circle and looking down. The woman wondered what it might be as there was an air of concern amongst the people, and she hoped that no one was lying hurt; the spectators were so tightly huddled that she couldn't make out what it was that was causing so much interest.

She came closer; it seemed that there was some puzzlement:

'Wot do yo' think it is?'

'I dunno. Wot do yo' think?'

'I never seen anythin' like it!'

'Nor me. Do yo' think it's safe?'

The woman's interest was piqued and she tried to see what the subject of the discussion was, but it was hard to get a good look. Eventually she managed to elbow her way under someone's arm and get her head into the middle of the circle. She looked down, and although she hadn't known what to expect, she certainly didn't think it would be this.

There, lying flat on the ground in between a daisy and a dandelion, was a shiny gold sovereign. The woman thought for a moment, then, wriggling her way out of the circle, she cried in a bold voice, 'Stand back! Stand back all of you, I don't want you to get burnt.'

The circle suddenly widened as everyone shuffled back four paces.

'Why?' said a voice. 'Do yo' know what it is then, missus?'

'I certainly do,' she said. 'Oh yes, I've seen a few of these before, and I'll be honest with you, no one knows where they come from, or how.'

All faces were turned towards her, all ears listening.

'This,' she paused dramatically, 'is a red-hot shilling.'

Everyone looked down, open mouthed. Of course! Once it was pointed out, it was obvious.

'Now, it can't be touched yet, obviously. And in my experience, these red-hot shillings take a while to cool down.'

Several of the listeners worked in a foundry, and they knew something about cooling times. There was a general nodding in agreement.

The woman was warming to her subject.

'And, of course, it will get to a temperature when it is no longer glowing but still hot enough to burn.'

More nodding from the foundry workers.

'I have a suggestion for you. I have plenty of time today, and I expect you have work to go to. So I will sit by the shilling and wait for it to cool while you go about your business. Then, when it is cool, I will take the shilling while you,' she took her purse from her pocket and removed a coin, 'share this shilling of mine between you.'

The oldest member of the group appointed himself leader and stepped forward to take the coin.

'That is very kind of yo' missus,' he said, and, holding up the shilling for all to see, he led the way back into town.

The woman settled down on the grass to wait, and when the last of the crowd had trailed out of sight, she picked up the gold sovereign, popped it in her purse and went on her way.

14

MODERN AND URBAN MYTHS

These little tales often fall into the category 'strange but true'; odd happenings that are passed on by word of mouth and on the Internet. They are told as factual, and while it's unusual to come across anyone who has personally witnessed the events in the story, there seem to be a large number of people who know someone who knows someone who was definitely there. It is probably not necessary to warn the reader that some of these tales may not be true.

THE SUTTON PARK FROGS

Sutton Park is an extensive area of heathland, woodland and lakes, just 6 miles north of Birmingham city centre. It's home to cattle and wild ponies, and there's even a donkey sanctuary. The Anglo-Saxon kings of Mercia established it as a Royal Forest, and there are still visible remains of the boundary banks and ditches. Later it became a Norman deer park, and eventually Henry VIII was persuaded by Sutton-born Bishop Vesey to grant the park as a gift to the people of Sutton Coldfield. Although the park is entirely surrounded by urban areas, it retains its wild character and it's big enough to make getting lost a distinct possibility.

The park is much loved and used by local residents as well as those from farther afield. One such resident was Sylvia Mowday, who, on 12 June 1954 was taking her young children, a girl and a boy, to a naval exhibition in the park.

Mrs Mowday said afterwards that she noticed the sky getting suddenly dark, and soon hail, or what she thought was hail, started falling from the sky. Her son commented that it wasn't hail, but frogs, and Sylvia Mowday saw that he was right, they were tiny baby frogs.

Her daughter had a small red umbrella, and she remembered the sound of the frogs thudding onto the umbrella and bouncing off. This went on for about five minutes and covered an area of 50 square yards. Mrs Mowday commented that the ground was so thick with the frogs that she and her children were afraid to move, for fear of treading on them.

I haven't been able to find any accounts from other witnesses of the Sutton Park shower of frogs, but certainly there are reports from across Europe of similar things happening – so maybe this story isn't a myth. Scientists have said that the downpour of frogs could have been caused by a tornado, whipping up the contents of a pond and carrying it until it became too heavy.

Alien Visitors

Fentham Road in Aston is a curving street of Victorian houses stretching from the A34 to the playing fields of King Edward VI School. A lady resident reported being visited by aliens on several occasions between 1956 and 1958. They showed off their advanced technology, taught her Venusian, and got her pregnant.

When the baby was born, he was called Matthew. It is not recorded, however, whether the name was chosen by his mother or his father(s). At some later point, the whole family disappeared. Swept off in a flying saucer, perhaps?

MARTIANS AND MINCE PIES

A woman living in Rowley Regis had just seen her husband off to work in his car in January 1979, when her eye was caught by a large orange sphere hovering near the driveway. Alarmed, she rushed back into the house, but she was overtaken by three tiny winged figures, wearing little goldfish-bowl-like helmets. They flew into the living room and alighted on the Christmas tree, which they began to shake with such vigour that the fairy was dislodged from the top.

The little creatures told the woman that they came 'from the sky' and, she later reported, they talked about Jesus and Tommy Steele. (In December 1979, Tommy Steele starred in a film where he played a broken toy that miraculously comes to life; perhaps the little aliens had advance knowledge of that fact. Or maybe they were reviewing his 1978 performance as Jack Point in Gilbert and Sullivan's 'The Yeomen of the Guard'?)

The woman went off to the kitchen and returned with a tray of mince pies, which she offered to her visitors (well, aren't we all desperate to get rid of lingering mince pies in January?). She must have been very happy to see them take one each. The creatures then left, flying off in their ship towards Oldbury or West Bromwich. Possibly they were in the mood for a game of footie with the Albion at The Hawthorns.

That's all there is of that story, so it just remains for us to hope that it took place before the 6th of January; everyone knows it's bad luck to have Christmas decorations up after Twelfth Night.

Ghostly Voice

A family were living near the site of the former Black Bat Mine. One day the daughter, 11-year-old Tracey, was listening to a home-recorded music tape. The music was interrupted by a crashing sound on the tape, followed by screaming and what sounded like a boy's voice saying, 'Is anybody down there?'

Tracey's mother Joyce said that the tape had been recorded some time previously, and there was nothing like that on the tape before. 'The ghostly voices suddenly appeared,' she said.

The family later found that the Black Bat Mine had been closed in 1883 after a roof collapsed, killing a number of men and boys.

The Chalk Symbols

In early 2006, groups of concerned residents in my home town of Walsall printed a number of simple leaflets and distributed them to householders in the area. The leaflets showed six drawings of symbols that were believed to be chalked onto houses by thieves to indicate to other interested parties whether or not a house was a good target.

The symbols purported to show whether a house was alarmed, whether it was worth burgling, whether it had already been burgled (if it hadn't, how would the thieves know if it was worth breaking in?) and, more chillingly, if the occupant was nervous and fearful or if she was a lone woman.

The West Midlands Police said they had no knowledge of any such symbols being in use, and neither had they received any

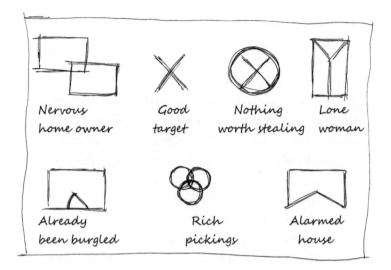

Nervous home owner

Good target

Nothing worth stealing

Lone woman

Already been burgled

Rich pickings

Alarmed house

reports of the symbols appearing on any houses. A Neighbourhood Watch co-ordinator warned against starting an unnecessary panic, adding that he had seen no evidence of the truth of this claim.

So it would seem that this is a fine example of the creation of a modern urban myth. With a little thought, it doesn't seem to hold water: why would thieves want to help other thieves in this random way, and why is there no symbol for what must be an important consideration for a thief – does the household include a dog?

But just in case, maybe we should all nip down to the pound shop and buy a pack of those big pavement chalks and draw a large circle enclosing a cross on the fronts of our houses. It's the symbol for 'Nothing worth stealing'.

THE MOTORCYCLIST

One moonless night three motorcylists were riding on the A45 near the National Exhibition Centre. They kept pace with each other for miles, but there came a point when the lead rider checked his mirrors and found that his mates had dropped a long way behind. At that moment, the street lights went out and it gave the rider an idea of a trick to play on the other two. He pulled over and switched off his lights, then turned his bike and rode the wrong way down the road. His idea was to ride in between his two friends in the darkness and scare them.

As he rode his bike, scarcely able to see where he was going in the deep gloom, he saw the two lights of the other bikes approaching him. Crouching in the saddle, he accelerated and aimed at the dead centre between the beams.

Too late, he realised that what he had taken to be the headlights of two motorbikes were actually the lights of a van, speeding towards him.

THE PRISON BREAK

In the 1850s, when Winson Green prison in Birmingham was only a few years old, prisoners dying there could be buried just outside the grounds. The man's body was placed in a coffin and was then sent down to the mortuary, where the caretaker nailed down the lid and buried the body in a grave dug by inmates.

When one of the prisoners heard of this procedure, it gave him an idea. He set about befriending the mortuary caretaker, finding opportunities when he could of helping him in small ways. In the few moments here and there when the prisoner was able to exchange words with the caretaker, he told him of the riches, in money and in jewels, that he had hidden away. He told him that he would be willing to share his wealth, enough for each of them to live in luxury, if the caretaker would help him to escape.

Eventually, the two men made a plan. The caretaker had duplicate keys cut, so that the prisoner could make his own way to the mortuary at night. The next time a man died, the prisoner would get into the coffin with the corpse. He would have with him a little food that he had saved, and matches and a candle in case the darkness was too much for him. The caretaker would nail down the lid and oversee the burial, then as soon as the prisoners had returned to their cells, he would dig up the coffin and the two men would make their escape to a new life.

The plan worked, up to a point. The prisoner heard in the exercise yard that there was to be a burial that night, so when the guard was distracted he slipped away and let himself into the mortuary. There, in the dim light, he could just make out the bulky shape of a coffin. Easing off the lid, he climbed inside and squeezed himself down next to the cold body.

Soon enough, he heard footsteps approaching, and the hard sound of nails being hammered home. There was a lurch as the coffin was lifted, a rocking motion as it was carried to the graveside and lowered in, then the thud of clods of earth falling on the lid. Then silence.

Waiting in the dark, the prisoner tried hard to stay calm, but he couldn't stop the panic rising. What if the caretaker took too long to dig him up? He didn't know how long the air in the coffin would last. Thinking it might help him to hold his nerve if he had a little light, he fumbled in his pocket for some matches and a stub of candle. He tried to strike a match, but his hands were shaking so much that he dropped the box. Feeling around him, the prisoner, after what seemed like an age, found a match, struck it and with a trembling hand lit the candle. He saw, for the first time, the face of the corpse.

It was the mortuary caretaker.

The Final Exam

In one of Birmingham's universities, fifty students were seated at their individual desks in the main hall. The exam invigilator instructed them to write their exam number on the top of the first page of their answer booklet, and reminded them not to identify themselves by name anywhere on their script. They then read out the examination rules – no talking or any other communication between candidates, all answers to be written from memory only with no use of notes of any kind, no writing before the start time or after the invigilator had indicated the end.

There was silence for the next three hours, broken only by the occasional rustle as a student turned over their exam paper. Towards the end of the time, the invigilator announced 'Five more minutes.'

One of the students, realising she had a lot more to say about the answer she was currently writing, started scribbling furiously, and she was so absorbed in getting down as many words as possible that she completely missed the call, 'Time's up. Pens down,' and she carried on writing until she suddenly realised that all the other students had left and the invigilator was approaching down the aisle, collecting up the papers.

The student offered him her paper with a smile, but he shook his head and said, 'I can't accept that. You were writing after I called time. You'll have to re-sit in six months.'

The student knew she couldn't do that; she had a job offer waiting. So she drew herself up, looked down her nose and said in a cold voice, 'Do you have any idea who I am?'

The invigilator looked her up and down with a sneer and said, 'No, I don't have any idea who you are, and I don't care either.'

The student said, 'Good!' She knocked all the exam papers out of his hand onto the floor, where she shoved her own paper amongst them, jumbled them all up, and ran off. She got an 'A'.

ANOTHER FINAL EXAM

In another Birmingham university, a student entering the exam room for the final exam of his course asked for two answer booklets. At the end of the exam, he left one of the booklets on his desk for the invigilator to collect and walked out with the other one under his arm. He hurried back to his room in the hall of residence, consulted his course notes and text books and wrote very thorough answers to the exam questions. He then posted the booklet with the answers in it to his mother.

A few days later, the same booklet arrived at the university. The student's mother had posted it back to the admin office, with a note to say that it had obviously been sent to her in error. The university authorities took pity on the student, and although it was not really within the rules, they accepted the exam paper, marked it and awarded an 'A'.

And the booklet that the student had left in the exam room to be collected? It simply said, 'Dear Mum, I have just finished my final exam and I think I've done quite well. I'll be home soon. Your loving son, Brian xxx'.

YET ANOTHER FINAL EXAM

In yet another Birmingham university, two students were nearing the end of their course. Throughout the three years they had both had the same approach to study. They didn't bother much at all with work, prioritising their social lives instead, and when an exam was imminent, they would 'pull an all-nighter' and cram furiously. With this strategy, they had just managed to scrape through. In spite of the obvious importance of the final exam, the students saw no reason to curtail the fun they were having; their last-minute exam prep had always seen them through before.

It was the day before the exam. The pair had spent most of the day lounging in the university coffee shop, and they were beginning to wonder if they ought to go and do a bit of preparation for the exam, when one of the young women on their course came in and spotted them.

'Hey guys! Want to come to a party? There's a whole gang of us going, it'll take our minds off tomorrow.'

At first the two students said they'd better not, they really needed to study. Their friend gave them the address in case they changed their minds, and she left. The students looked at one another, both with the same thought.

'I suppose we could just go for an hour,' said one.

'Just a couple of drinks won't hurt,' said the other, and off they went.

The following afternoon, the pair of them blearily drifted into consciousness feeling like death. They looked at the clock, and then at each other with horror. They had not only missed the start of the exam, they had missed the end of it as well. They needed a plan.

Two hours and three cups of coffee later, they had one. They went together to see their head of department, to explain their absence and to plead to be allowed to sit the exam.

The professor invited them into her office and listened patiently to their story.

'I had a phone call late last night,' said one, 'about my dear old aunt who lives in Dudley. She'd been taken ill and rushed to hospital, so I had to go over there.'

'And I had to navigate,' said the second. 'And we were there all night.'

'That's right, but on our way back this morning, we got a flat tyre. Then we found the spare was flat as well, so we had to try and find a garage, and by the time we got back here we'd missed the exam.'

The professor nodded. 'And how is your aunt?'

'She pulled through. She's on the mend now.'

The professor agreed to allow them to sit the exam and told them to come back tomorrow. When they returned, they were shown into separate rooms to sit the exam. Turning over the exam paper, they both saw only one question:

'Which tyre?'

THE BIRMINGHAM VAMPIRE

In 2005, in Glen Park Road, Ward End, a man attacked another man, biting him. When neighbours rushed to help, the attacker bit them too, with one woman having chunks taken out of her hand. The *Birmingham Mail* was inundated with calls reporting similar incidents in the Saltley, Alum Rock and Small Heath areas of the city.

The 'vampire's' ploy, apparently, was to knock on people's front doors and when they opened the door, to grab them and bite them.

The police, however, stated that no such incidents had been reported to them, and they said they thought it was probably just an urban myth. It's in the right chapter then!

The priest of a Catholic church in Small Heath had the last word. He said that he had heard the rumours when visiting the barber's. He was asked if he believed in vampires and he said no.

'I'm not worried though,' he said. 'I've got a lot of crucifixes in the house.'

BIBLIOGRAPHY

BOOKS

Brown, Richard S., *The Folklore Superstitions and Legends of Birmingham and the West Midlands*, Westwood Press 1992

Fanous, Samuel, *A Conspiracy of Ravens*, Bodleian Library, 2014

Freeman, John (ed. Harold Parsons), *Freeman's Black Country Folk*, Black Country Society, 1970

Gough, T.H., *Black Country Stories*, Hudson, 1934

Grice, Frederick, *Folk Tales of the West Midlands*, Thomas Nelson & Sons, 1952

Hill, Stan, *More Black Country Humour Tales and Verse*, The Black Country Society, 1994

Homer, Winston and Parsons, Harold, *Black Country Humour*, Black Country Society, 1980

Lyons, Amy, *Black Country Sketches*, Kates Hill Press, 2012, reprinted from a 1901 publication

Palmer, Roy, *Britain's Living Folklore*, David & Charles, 1991

Palmer, Roy, *The Folklore of the Black Country*, Logaston Press, 2007

Parker, Douglas, *Aynuk & Ayli's Black Country Joke Book*, Broadside, 1984

Raven, Jon, *Tales from Aynuk's Black Country*, Broadside, 1978

Raven, Jon, *Stories, Customs, Superstitions, Tales, Legends and Folklore of the Black Country and Staffordshire*, Broadside, 1986

Raven, Jon, *The Book of the Black Country*, Broadside, 1988

Raven, Jon, *The Folklore and Songs of the Black Country Colliers*, Broadside, 1990

Raven, Michael, *West Midlands' Ballads*, Michael Raven, 2008

Tump, Aristotle, *Tales of Terror Volume Two*, Bugle Publications, 1985

WEBSITES

www.blackcountrymuse.com/folklore.htm

www.birminghammail.co.uk/news/midlands-news/21-things-you-not-know-7418256

www.birminghammail.co.uk/whats-on/whats-on-news/24-reasons-you-would-never-10846456

www.themodernantiquarian.com/latest/0/5/2242

www.blackcountrysociety.co.uk/articles/b&briots1.htm

https://billdargue.jimdo.com/placenames-gazetteer-a-to-y/places-g/gilbertstone/

Society *for*
Storytelling

Since 1993, The Society for Storytelling has championed the ancient art of oral storytelling and its long and honourable history – not just as entertainment, but also in education, health, and inspiring and changing lives. Storytellers, enthusiasts and academics support and are supported by this registered charity to ensure the art is nurtured and developed throughout the UK.

Many activities of the Society are available to all, such as locating storytellers on the Society website, taking part in our annual National Storytelling Week at the start of every February, purchasing our quarterly magazine Storylines, or attending our Annual Gathering – a chance to revel in engaging performances, inspiring workshops, and the company of like-minded people.

You can also become a member of the Society to support the work we do. In return, you receive free access to Storylines, discounted tickets to the Annual Gathering and other storytelling events, the opportunity to join our mentorship scheme for new storytellers, and more. Among our great deals for members is a 30% discount off titles from The History Press.

For more information, including how to join, please visit

www.sfs.org.uk